Percival
and the Presence of God

More Titles from Chaosium

Pendragon™ Fiction

The Arthurian Companion
The Bear of Britain (forthcoming)
To the Chapel Perilous (forthcoming)

Call of Cthulhu® Fiction

Robert Bloch's Mysteries of the Worm
Cthulhu's Heirs
The Shub-Niggurath Cycle
Encyclopedia Cthulhiana
The Azathoth Cycle
The Book of Iod
Made in Goatswood
The Dunwich Cycle
The Disciples of Cthulhu Second Edition
The Cthulhu Cycle
The Necronomicon
The Xothic Legend Cycle
The Nyarlathotep Cycle
The Hastur Cycle 2nd Edition

Pendragon™ Fiction

Percival
and the Presence of God

by
JIM HUNTER

INTRODUCTION BY RAYMOND H. THOMPSON,
SERIES EDITOR

A Chaosium Book
1997

Percival and the Presence of God is published by Chaosium, Inc. First published in 1978 by Faber and Faber Limited (U.K.).

©1978, 1997 by Jim Hunter; all rights reserved.

Cover art ©1997 by Ed Org; all rights reserved.

Cover layout by Charlie Krank. Edited by Raymond H. Thompson, Ph.D. Interior layout and additional editorial by Janice Sellers. Proofreading by Elaine Fuller. Editor-in-Chief Lynn Willis.

Please address questions and comments concerning this book, as well as requests for free notices of Chaosium publications, by mail to Chaosium, Inc., 950 56th St., Oakland, CA 94608-3136, U.S.A. Also visit our web page at:

http://www.sirius.com/~chaosium/chaosium/html

FIRST PAPERBACK EDITION

1 2 3 4 5 6 7 8 9 10

Chaosium Publication 6201. Published in July 1997.

ISBN 1-56882-097-6

Printed in Canada.

Introduction

This century has witnessed a dramatic growth in the popularity of fiction based on Arthurian legend. From a mere trickle at the outset, barely noticeable amidst the torrent of Arthurian poems and plays, it has swelled to its present pre-eminence. This growth, moreover, is remarkable not only for the number of books involved, but also for their scope, ranging from historical novels set in the distant past of Dark Age Britain to science fiction set in an alien future; from the familiar circumstances of contemporary experience to the wondrous world of fantasy; from the brooding suggestiveness of Gothic romance to the explicitness of the erotic novel; from the anguish of the tragic mode, to the inspiration of the heroic, to the exuberance of the comic.

To those of us who have learned to love the legend, this growth is most welcome, offering as it does a wealth of choice. The avid Arthurian reader soon discovers, however, that it has one frustrating consequence: many novels have fallen out of print. Given the economics of the modern publishing industry, this situation is inescapable. This recognition, nevertheless, provides little consolation to readers reduced either to trying to borrow books on interlibrary loan from libraries that are increasingly reluctant to incur the cost of sending off any material, let alone something irreplaceable; or else to combing the shelves of second-hand bookstores on the slim chance they might find what they are looking for. Under these circumstances, we are proud to inaugurate the *Pendragon*™ series of Arthurian fiction, which is designed to make available again some of the best Arthurian novels ever written.

The novel chosen to begin the series is Jim Hunter's *Percival and the Presence of God*. First published in England in 1978, it was given limited circulation in hard cover, and few if any copies reached North America. Those who acquired it clearly recognised its merits, for it has become a very scarce book indeed. My own admiration for Hunter's novel dates from the research I conducted for *The Return from Avalon: A Study of the Arthurian Legend in Modern Fiction* (1985). There I included it among that handful of historical novels that 'succeed in evoking the heroic spirit of the Arthurian story as well as giving it life and immediacy' (73).

Percival and the Presence of God has the distinction, unique so far in Arthurian legend, of being a Christian existential novel. In it Percival tells the story of his dual quest: first, to become a knight at King Arthur's court; then, after his failure to ask the vital question when he witnesses the Grail procession at the castle of the fisher-lord, to return and correct his mistake. This is the traditional tale, first told by Chrétien de Troyes in the twelfth century, though details are used sparingly and adapted freely to suit the needs of Hunter's novel. Here Percival rescues Whiteflower and comes across the Grail Castle, but he never does find King Arthur, despite a prolonged and diligent search. Indeed, at the end of the novel he confesses, 'I no longer believe in Arthur, it being all I can manage to believe in God.'

What distinguishes Hunter's account is the credibility of the characters and the world in which they live. As the author himself has observed, he set out to 'write something set in the past, but so vivid that it felt as if you were out there in the wind with it.' Yet while the setting is realised in stark and graphic detail, it remains strangely elusive, for there is nothing to place it firmly in any particular century. It has a timeless and even otherworldly quality despite its realism. Not only is this an appropriate setting in which to search for King Arthur and the Holy Grail, but it also shifts the focus to the characters who move through it, especially the narrator.

Percival recalls his youthful adventures well after the events themselves, but since experience brings no clear answers to the major questions in his life, he remains as perplexed at the end as he was at the outset. His narrative thus preserves the immediacy of his reactions: he is no better able to understand the behaviour of Whiteflower, or the fisher-lord, or even his own compulsions, in retrospect than he was earlier. Thus we relive with him such traumatic events as the recovery and cremation of the corpse of his beloved mentor Mansel, his love-making with Whiteflower after he defeats her attackers, the agony of the fisher-lord at the Grail feast, and his own journey to the brink of death, trapped by fallen timbers in a ruined chapel.

Although such experiences may seem far removed from ordinary life, Percival's baffled reaction to them makes it clear that Hunter is exploring a twentieth-century consciousness as illuminated by the past. The questions to which he seeks answers touch all of us deeply, concerned as they are with basic issues of life and death: how do we cope with the pain of separation from loved ones? Will we be given a second chance to rectify past mistakes? Why are some taken and others spared? What is the purpose of suffering? Assailed by doubt about the existence not only of Arthur but of God Himself, Percival persists in his quest. He is driven not just by habit and stubbornness, but by a compulsion beyond his understanding, a need to find a deeper purpose to life than this world offers. He thus becomes trapped by his own destiny and, when he eventually finds what he thinks is Arthur's castle, he is almost destroyed by it.

That a modern realistic writer like Hunter should draw upon traditional material for so disturbing a journey of discovery is less surprising than it might seem. Myth and legend have always been concerned with such profound issues, and they lie at the heart of the Arthurian cycle, in stories of Arthur's conception and birth, the rise and fall of his kingdom, and his mysterious passing. Among the most fascinating of these stories is that of the Grail quest in which are combined chivalric, Christian, and pagan elements. In Hunter's novel, the first two provide the motivating forces for Percival's quests, first to find Arthur, then the fisher-lord. As in medieval romance, the pagan elements are more shadowy, but they can be discerned not only in the fertility symbolism of the Grail ceremony, but also in the triple manifestation of the Mother Goddess as maiden, mother, and crone: the mad girl who finds Percival when he is trapped in the ruined chapel; the almost mythic figure of Whiteflower; and the old woman who mocks the hero during the parody scene in the hall.

The integration of such disparate elements in a novel that is predominantly realistic demonstrates the value and importance of Arthurian tradition as a source of inspiration for modern authors. They in their turn enrich the tradition, recreating it anew for another generation of readers and writers alike. This process of enrichment ensures that Arthurian legend will continue to fascinate as it has already done down through the ages, and that we can look forward to sharing more journeys of discovery like that of Hunter's Percival, 'so vivid that it felt as if you were out there in the wind with it.' As in the great English medieval poem *Sir Gawain and the Green Knight*, the wind that blows is a cold one, testing our human frailty. It also reminds us to what heights the human spirit can ascend, however remote and unattainable the goal may appear.

Enjoy the experience!

Raymond H. Thompson
February, 1997

When Bonhoeffer says that God wants us to live as if
there were no God I suspect he is misusing words. ...
We are simply here. And if there is any kind of sense
or unity in human life, and the dream of this does not
cease to haunt us, it is of some other kind and must
be sought within a human experience which has nothing outside it.

Iris Murdoch

1

'For the wolves,' the man kept repeating.

He stood, wide-legged, wide-armed, facing me, swinging from the hips, flapping his hand and his sword at the corpses either side of him.

'These are for the wolves,' he shouted.

The bone of his skull swelled out, great polished lintels above the eyes. Those eyes narrowed and widened, narrowed and widened, unceasingly; some matter of defective vision, an effort to see clearly, but it seemed like possible mockery. At least some dull insult. The teeth at the right of his mouth were stove in, from some injury long ago, molars skewed inwards, the line of the gums contorted. Suddenly one could pity him.

Then he laughed, baying the broken mouth open wider.

'The . . . wolves!' he mouthed, guying the words, as if to an idiot or—this was the point—to a child.

I passed the weight of my sword to my left hand and with the right hit him, across the jaw.

He staggered, half thrown by the blow, half lurching away from further blows. The other men caught what had happened, lifted their heads and saw him, as he slewed in the mud, wheeling his arms, to keep his body upright. Then he fell, his flung-out left hand tearing against broken bone, deep to the wrist in blood. The back of his head slapped momentarily against the corpse's collapsed chest. He coughed with horror, and pitched forward again on to one knee. He shook his head: cords of black hair joggling. Where he touched the back of his hand to his cheek, testing the bone, he left it blotched with viscousness of blood, but seemed not to realize.

I stood still. About me the other men stood, leaning upright. Through my hair, at the side of my right eye, I glimpsed one man stepping forward. Out of sight, behind him, there would be two others. It was important, however, not to look at any, except the man I had knocked down.

'Up,' I muttered. 'Get up.'

It was also important not to lift my sword.

The man got up, slipping and nearly falling again. The blood of the dead man clung to his left cheek, the whole outer arm, the hand, and the side of his knee. Watching him I guessed that, though he would slop the hand and face free at the river, and cleanse that part of him, the dried blood on the sleeve would be on him all winter.

'Listen to me,' I said.

He lifted his head and stared. The eyes, in that pathetic fluctuation, were blank of meaning. The mouth, still half-open, the twisted teeth there half-visible, was weighed downwards at the sides, in resentment.

I felt sick, but certain. I turned slightly now, looking behind me at the others. 'Listen to me every man,' I said loudly.

'No one of these dead,' I said, 'is to be left for the wolves.'

I watched: there were faint movements. An old man lowered his head.

'How many have we killed?'

They glanced about them. Nobody answered.

'Ranalph,' I called. 'Search, and count the corpses. From here,' I gestured, 'to their fire. And,' I turned the other way, 'from here to the river. Then tell me the number, the exact number. Begin.'

Without urgency, Ranalph moved, heavy-footed, his one leg longer than the other. I trusted him. The men began to drop their heads, murmuring to one another.

'No man,' I shouted suddenly, 'should be left for wolves. Not the murderer of your mother. Not the child-stealer. Not the wretch guilty of sacrilege. Listen, and learn this. My enemy is a man. If I kill him as a man, I consign him as a man. That is the code. I bury him.'

I glanced at the water-meadows, and the deep mud.

'Or I burn him. These we shall burn. Before nightfall we shall have built a pyre. Over there, where their own fire was during these days. We shall burn them all at dusk. In the morning I shall count the skulls.'

My voice sounded thin and impossibly young, in the wide air, after the days within the house. I pressed it to be stronger and harder.

'That is the right way,' I said. 'Isn't it?'

A mistake, to appeal to their opinion. They shifted together.

'It is the right way,' I cried, more quickly. 'Think. In a time to come I or you may be killed by enemies. That will not be a disgrace. Nor were these deaths disgraceful. Nor shall we consign them disgracefully, to hogs or wolves. That is the code.'

'My lord,' said a man near me. He waited for my nod, then spoke on. 'My lord, the wealth of these dead isn't theirs. It's ours.' He grinned, challenging me. 'By your code even, I reckon.'

I swung my free hand across my chest, edging it for a backswipe. Then lowered it slowly, by my side.

'The pillaging may continue,' I said. 'Clothing; jewels; arms. Ranalph will collect all and present it in the keep at midday. Your lady will share out the spoils. Each of you will benefit.'

Relief spread across their faces.

'Carry on,' I said. 'You may strip the bodies.'

My own best spear, upright still in the reeds like a waymark, held pinned in swamped mud the body of Gagreth himself, who had led the siege. It had been one of the finest throws of my life; certainly the most crucial. I touched the still rigid shaft, dedicating the shot in my mind; not to my mother or Mansel, but to the lady Whiteflower. Then I freed it from the corpse. To do this I had to sling my sword in its girdle loop, ungainly, and drag with both hands upwards and outwards. The spear had driven through cheek and throat, breaking the jawbone, and as it was withdrawn it locked, in the smashed bone. With the last cracking wrench more blood flooded the cavity and continued to come.

I snatched and broke a handful of reeds and wiped from my spear the blood and fragments of bone; and the fresh glint returned. Then I looked again at Gagreth.

His own men had already taken from his body its best possessions. I remembered, after I had speared his head and seen him fall among the reeds, seeing two of his fellows work their way, keeping low, towards this place. And for a few moments I had glimpsed their heads and backs, as they knelt there. I had thought that they were ministering to the dying leader, in surgery or shrift; and had held my fire. But now the great silver clasp from above Gagreth's breastbone, which I had glimpsed at a distance several times, was gone; so was his fur; and two fingers of his left hand had been cut off, with their rings. His sword had gone, his gauntlets, his boots. The spear itself, perhaps, they had feared to touch, since it had brought such a death; or, since to remove it one had needed to stand upright and use full strength, they might not have cared to expose themselves there as targets.

Turning away, I lifted the spear above my shoulder, bouncing it a little in the hand. Its sleek point poised ahead of me, in the sunlight. Passing the nearest men I told them they might strip Gagreth's corpse, and carry it to the place of the fire.

I went to meet Ranalph, returning from his hobbling survey of the field. There were eleven bodies, he told me. I gave him instructions for the building of the pyre, and the collection and sharing of spoils. Nearly three times my age, he listened with simple nods, unquestioning.

I walked, each pace sinking in the wet meadow, not towards the house but towards the river, away from the others. Their voices, shouting occasionally to each other, thinned with the distance. I moved with the plash of my boots, the brushed reeds, the small sounds of my clothing and weapons. I had it in mind to rest on the river bank awhile, out of sight of the others, in the sun and the sound of water; as I would have done by the river at home, while Mansel fished, or with no one at all.

From near the river-bank there were sounds of an animal, among the grasses; and then, quickly, they were recognizable not as animal but as human. There was a wounded man there. As I moved towards the noise it stopped, or almost stopped. This was what must have happened when Ranalph approached, on his survey: the man had feigned death and been missed. Then, when I was almost over him, the pain forced sound out of him again.

He hadn't the strength to make much of a cry; but it was as if his spirit rasped against its crushed prison—as if the sound was of friction rather than voice. His face, half in the grass, was twisted back from the mouth and eyes, like a mask. His eyeball tried to see me.

It was the man Saglar had brought down, before himself being killed at the main area of fighting. But Saglar had not quite killed him. I stooped, tugging at his shoulder and thigh, and rolled him on to his back. The man screamed, with little voice but with the agony of his life.

He should not have been alive. Saglar's sword had opened him across the midriff, terrible to see; and, after tearing the lower clothing aside, had severed his genitals from his abdomen.

In my life I had never fainted; but I had seen boys, and at least once a man, do so; and I recognized in the featheriness of my mind the risk of that disgrace. More important than the avoidance of disgrace, though, was the need to release the mutilated man from his suffering. I breathed heavily, with mouth wide open, looking momentarily away from him to the river, as I lifted my sword from its hanging. As I swung it above the man's neck his eyes jutted with horror; the half-opened body twisted in a hoarse protest—he wanted to live, imagining that he could. Into the one chop downwards I put all the power of my arms.

At the water's edge, where the bank shielded me from the scavengers, I threw down my sword, laying the spear beside it. I stood above the moving river, watching the water, waiting for the featheriness to die inside me.

The autumn sun, low and sidelong, dazzled on the water surface. I closed my eyes to slits, listening to the quiet swirl of the water.

When I knelt to wash, a muscle at the back of my right knee ached. I washed my face and arms, repeatedly; and cupped the cold water against my closed eyes, in the palms of my hands. Then, in wiping my face with my fingers, I rolled my fingertips against the fuzz of my beard, as I always did, by instinct. The moustache was there, more or less, I could stroke it sleek against the skin. On the cheeks and chin, though, there was still only a pale fur.

It didn't matter. I lay on the river bank, in the sun. It didn't matter, much. I thought: I've no doubts of my manhood. I am eighteen years old. I now throw—by God's kindness—better than any man, of any age, I have met or heard of. And today, by God's kindness, I killed Gagreth, the most serious enemy I have encountered. Let the beard come late, if it has to.

The lady Whiteflower would be with her chaplain still, giving thanks. In a while I would go to the chapel myself. And then busy myself with the men, and the spoils.

A shout came from nearer by. I half-sat up on one elbow, taking my sword.

Through the grasses of the bank I saw two of the scavengers, one calling the other. He stood over the mutilated body whose life I had finished. They both stooped over the body. One laughed. Then they lifted it between them, and set off back to the others.

I sat up, and began to massage my right knee, fingering and working through the pain there. A year ago Mansel would have done this for me, kneeling beside me, his black-haired hands driving the muscle. We would have been talking about the day's action, which he would surely have approved. I wondered how Mansel would have spoken to Saglar today, about that violation of an enemy, supposing that Saglar had lived. Or how he would have spoken to the others. It was possible, after all, that any of them might have done the same, that now by the pyre they were mutilating Gagreth's corpse, and those of his fellows, in the same way.

What would Gagreth have committed upon my body, if the victory had been his?

I flexed the knee and straightened it, then stood up, bending the knee once or twice again. I turned my back to the sun and looked towards the house. The men were returning, in twos and threes. And in and out of the main gate, women and children were freely passing, as they had been unable to do for days. Somewhere within was the lady of the house; and now she would be my lady.

I did want to be her lord. I wanted today's heroism to be the first of many. I wanted to seek Arthur; and to find him. I wanted to belong to others, to be less my own: I understood that a child is selfish and an adolescent lonely, and I wanted to be beyond these.

Yet I was reluctant to leave that quiet place, by the clear sound of the moving water, with the mild sun on my back.

My sword, on the grass, was still dulled with blood. I stooped, stiffly, closed my fingers round the hilt, and lifted it in front of my eyes. I turned towards the sunlight, and added the other hand to support the weight. I revolved it in my hands. Then, stooping again, I tore grass, and wiped and polished the blade slowly from end to end.

I wished I was in the sun, beside a quiet river, with Mansel near me, fishing; and my mother, half a mile away, preparing soup; and mountains against the sky.

2

Standing at the foot of her couch, I said:

'They won't come again until the spring, my lady. They lost too many today. At dusk we'll be burning twelve of them.'

Whiteflower's lips, without voice, repeated the number. The lips were drawn forward to form the word, her cheeks momentarily hollowed. Watching my face, she nodded slowly; then smiled suddenly and held out her hand.

'Perhaps, my lord, they'll never come again.'

She lowered her hand to the couch, indicating that I should sit there, by her feet. 'You may become a legend to them,' she said.

I laughed. A little uneasily, I sat where she directed.

She sat up, her eyes amused.'"The giant Percival, who crushed six men in each hand.". . . Yes ! That's the way legends grow.'

I glanced towards her, hardly smiling, reluctant to be mocked; and looked away at the room. It was the biggest private chamber I had ever seen, at that time: as big in area as most houses in my village; from one end to the other may have been thirty feet.

'Wouldn't you like to become a legend, my lord?'

'Not in a pack of lies like that.'

'Honourable. The interesting stories are the false ones, however. A story of what has in fact happened is trivial, it's outside us. Legends have something to say. And,' her voice changed towards amusement, 'they're part of the code. Are they not?'

'Sometimes,' I said quietly.

At table in the recent days I had talked too much, about my journey and my hopes. Her smiles, and those of the older men, had seemed sympathetic; but it had exposed me. I had failed to remember the abbot's advice: to let others lead, in matters of talk, particularly among strangers.

Whiteflower was smiling at me, turning away from me and slackening back into her crimson pillows. To smile at me was one thing. To smile at the code was another, particularly when I had just saved her, and her house.

'Yes, it is true,' I said, louder. My voice probably sounded raw and uncontrolled. I didn't want to be angry with her. 'It is true we learn from the legends of heroes. They can be important, and they shouldn't be laughed at.'

'I'm sorry.'

'Besides,' I said, to lighten it, 'the giants are always twice as big as me.'

'And ugly.' She laughed. 'And stupid.'

'And in all the best legends they lose.'

'To the code-hero. Yes. Today, my lord, you weren't giant, but giant-killer: the boy with the spear.'

Blood in my cheeks and throat.

I looked at my own hands, the hairless wrists. It was true that she was six years older than me, and true that my beard was late. But they were man's hands.

She knew I was hurt. She moved towards me on the couch and touched my arm, letting her hand run down to my wrist; turning the wrist towards herself, she made me look at her.

'Oh, my lord Percival,' she said—and her voice had the gravity of her recent fear—'I owe you much thanks.'

Stillness sealed the words between us. Then I nodded and said, rather stiffly, 'It was an honour.'

She lifted the back of her hand towards me, her eyes moving between my eyes and her hand. I raised it to my lips as I was meant to. Lady out of knights' dreams. As I kissed it she pressed the back of her hand up, against my mouth, for the time it takes to breathe.

I stood up, and stepped slowly away from her. My sword lay on a chest, perhaps a hundred years old, in the fan of light from a window. I touched my fingers to the ornamentation of the hilt, half-waiting to be told to go; and stooped to look out of the window. Behind me I heard Whiteflower raise herself and leave the couch. I glanced back, in case she came across to me, but she passed to her table and her mirror.

From the window I could look out over the marsh-grass and mud where we had fought. Beyond, the river was seen winding into the forest, and in the furthest distance were the hills through which I had journeyed.

Everything was filtered golden. Though it was not long past midday, the men building the pyre cast substantial shadows. The day's sunlight seemed symbolic, God's light, after the days of siege. And in this serenity the coming of winter too seemed heralded most graciously.

'Without you, my lord,' Whiteflower said suddenly, 'I should have been raped; probably many times over. And then, with luck, killed.'

I straightened from the window, and looked at her. She was standing before her mirror, touching her neck and collarbones with both hands. She glanced over her shoulder at me. 'Isn't that true?'

'I think so.'

Of course, she had been afraid.

'My lady,' I said, watching her fingers at her own throat, the little fingers playing with links in the chain below her chin, 'you shouldn't mock the code.'

Her hands stopped. 'Have I?'

'It seemed like it,' I said gently. I walked slowly away from her, down the length of the room.

'Well, I have every cause to respect the code; and to respect you.'

'I know it isn't perfect,' I said. 'There are things it doesn't give us any guidance with—like what to do about your dying parent, or how to run an estate. And of course some of the legends are unlikely; but we learn from them.'

'Surely,' she said. 'And you have certainly learnt.'

I nodded. 'Almost everything I know.'

Whiteflower took from the couch a crimson cushion, and dropped it to the floor beside me. 'Will you sit by me?' she said.

My slight hesitation immediately seemed ungracious. I crossed quickly, belatedly; and sat cross-legged on the cushion, the back of my head against the couch. I felt too like a page-boy for comfort. Yet we were reaching towards each other already, in our words.

The muscle behind my right knee had stiffened, and gave me some pain. It was strange to have come so fresh from battle, to a crimson cushion. All the time we were both aware that death had been near to us. The pain of the muscle was gladdening, speaking of life and victory.

'You were brought up in the code,' she said quietly.

'Yes. I was fortunate.'

'I should offer up masses for your tutor's soul.'

'He doesn't need them.' I bowed my head forward, touched my fingertips to my temples. 'He was the best of men.'

'He lived by the code?'

'Utterly.'

Her hand came among my hair. To my own surprise I leant my head sharply back, strengthening her caress, as a cat does. Down the back of my head, down the nape of the neck, back up to the crown, and down again: she had found the place of tension in me. Her small knuckles played and nudged into the hotness behind my ears. Was I a page-boy to her? I reached up behind my head and held her wrist; but not to hold it away from me. Then we were still.

'What was his name?'

'Mansel.'

'And he was a knight?'

'Of course. He had been trained by one who had been with Arthur.' I twisted my head upwards, to look at her. 'You understand what that means?'

That hollowing of her cheeks, her trick of sucking them in as she nodded, her eyes already on me.

'Doesn't it impress you?'

Whiteflower's shoulders lifted slightly, and fell again. She drew her hand away from my neck, slipping the wrist through my fingers, and sat back. She stroked instead her own gown, gold and green, her eyes there. She said: 'How did he die?'

'He was ambushed by petty robbers, in a high pass. . . . Ignorant men. They had no idea what a life they were cutting short.'

I saw Mansel laughing against the windy sky, holding the spear towards me.

'His knighthood meant nothing to them. They left him naked.' I crossed myself, shutting my eyes; but I wished to tell her. 'I found his body, after three days; it was covered in snow.'

Without opening my eyes, I lifted my face a little, against the calm air of the room: I too might have been dead, by this hour.

Above me Whiteflower moved on the couch; she leant down and kissed my forehead, holding my head in her hands, with her hair slipping against my cheek.

In my brain I saw Mansel's smile drying and dying on his face, his eyes reaching to mine, puz-

zled. In my brain, as when dreaming, I couldn't
move towards him.

Whiteflower had risen. I opened my eyes on a
bright widening slant of light from the window
which overlooked the battleplace. Dust spiralling
endlessly in the lighted air. For a moment I felt as
if in a place of desolation.

I turned, hearing a sound at the doorway.
Quietly, with both hands, the lady Whiteflower
was lifting a heavy wooden bolt across her door.
The slight scraping brought sound back to me. A
cart was creaking, from down towards the river,
and people out there were calling to each other.
The commerce of the region was starting up
again. All afternoon, provisions would arrive at
the main gate.

Somewhere at the back of the house I recognized a drinking song. In an hour or two, half the
men who had fought beside me this morning
would be in coma.

Whiteflower was crossing the room towards
me. I got up, with a feeling of scree collapsing
under my feet, welling about my ankles, a whole
mountainside spilling me towards the valleys.
The cheeks were again drawn in a little, in the
way which made her look so young; and hollow-
ness between her legs, as she moved in the silks.
I turned away, looking toward the window. In my
ears rocks thudded and burst down the gullies
below me: Mansel descending alongside and a little behind me, shouting words which the moving
mountain lost.

'Is it the code that makes you spin away?'

I stood by the low window, biting my breath
in, my body in warm sunlight from the waist

down. Weakly I said, not looking at her: 'The code doesn't approve discourtesy. But—' I tried to laugh—'it does tell me to be mistrustful of ladies who bolt the door from inside once one is with them.' I turned back to her, smiling with unsteady lips. 'In the legends that's enough to convict you of sorcery.'

She laughed, seated on the couch; but she was not calm either. From below us, somewhere in the house, the men's voices heaved in the chorus of a bawdy catch.

'My lord is free to leave as he pleases. The bolt isn't magicked.'

Indeed I could cross the room now, move the unmagic bolt, and leave, by the stairs and the inner yard, to ride away this day or the next. That would conserve me, leave me unaltered.

The song, below, came to its shouting end, followed by cheering. The voices fell back gradually.

It was clear that I would not leave. Whiteflower held out both hands to me; I went to her, taking them in mine. She did not rise, but drew me close to her and lowered her head against our four locked hands drawn together at my waist, like a heraldic representation. I opened my mouth to breathe, looking over her head at the wall of the room.

She said: 'Some parts of goodness have nothing to do with the code.'

I couldn't speak. I turned my head aside, hot-faced; in front of me our hands still clasped, tugging a little at each other.

'When the code gets in where it has no place—'

'It has a place everywhere.'

'In that case God help us.'

'I pray he will.'

She pulled my hands suddenly down towards her, making me brace my shoulders to stay upright. I smiled, but was unable to look steadily at her. She leant back, laughing a little, then broke free, twisting her hands away and out, the silks falling back from her wrists and lower arms. She swung her hair back with a twist of the head.

'Did your tutor encourage laughter, my lord?'

'Not particularly,' I said, resisting her. 'But he laughed himself.'

'But it isn't part of the code?'

'It isn't excluded.'

Our eyes were angry with each other. Yet again I swung away from her. From the chest I picked up the heavy sword, turning its blade in the light and watching it, to avoid watching her.

'Look. I am young,' I said. 'I understand that much of the deepest experience I still lack. But to know me, you must know that I have to follow the code. It's not a caprice, it's necessary.'

I put the sword down, its weight sounding on the hollow wood.

'Maybe when I was only thirteen or fourteen I was drawn by glamour. I loved the idea of heroism in the name of God. You, my lady, treat me as if I were still like that, a boy, dreaming.'

She was still, and I didn't look at her.

'I follow the code now because it *has* to be followed. Because of what I see of men without the code.'

I looked out to the marshes, ducking. 'Before Saglar was killed today,' I began.

Whiteflower gave a small cry. I turned, watched her cross herself, looking down at the floor. 'I didn't know Saglar was dead. He was a good servant.'

'Perhaps. Before he was killed, he took a victim; mutilated him, in the primitive way; and left him still living.'

She turned her face away from me.

'That was your good servant,' I said, my voice thick.

Dark waters in my brain, and the muscle in my knee aching. I stepped unevenly to a small carved Christ-on-the-cross, which she kept hanging from a wall-peg. I said:

'The code is what we must have, to draw us away from the beast. Saglar in time of peace was a good servant, you tell me: a tolerable, comfortable man. I expect he laughed, and loved. . . . In war, in test, that comfortable life can prove to be only a life of the animal. The code doesn't endorse it. Codeless men, you said, would have raped you. Tonight your own men would have left their own victims to wolves: I had to knock a man down, to club them into humanity. Even so they'll burn the dead more from fear of me than any better reason.'

I closed my eyes, weary, in front of the crucifix. She would not love me, for such a harangue.

Below us I could hear again the singing; slack, easy.

'I hear in your words the words of your tutor.'

'Yes.'

'My tutor was my husband.'

She was brushing a pillow smooth with her fingers, straightening the threads of its fringe.

'He married me when I was fifteen. He was ten years the older. We lived for nearly five years together."

'Now he is a knight? With Arthur?'

'Not personally. He had never travelled so far. Like you, he was educated in the direct tradition. One day,' she twisted a corner of the pillow, 'he set out on the Grail-search. Alone. It's something they nearly all do, apparently, at some time. . . . You have heard of the Grail?'

I half-laughed. 'Of course.'

'So, he set out. Four years ago at New Year. And the longest any man is known to have sought the Grail and returned is twenty months. He is dead, somewhere.'

'It's not certain.'

'I think it is certain. In a bear's cave, or beneath a tall cliff, or starved on a mountain. Somewhere, he is dead. He was killed in heroic combat with a magic king—it may be. Or butchered in a mud hut by codeless men.'

'He may yet return. You should pray, always.'

'Pray, I've prayed. Dead or alive, it's four years.' She lifted her head. 'In the end the code took him.'

'That has made you bitter.'

'Isn't it cause enough? But I couldn't love a codeless man. I accept all you say: the code protects us from ourselves. Only, I would rather see it as an outer frame, preserving freedom within.'

I smiled. 'Now you're using his words.'

'No, he didn't talk about his beliefs. That's for the immature.'

I stared at her.

'I beg your pardon,' she said. Colour darkened in her face.

I had to clear my throat, then my voice still shivered. 'I'll see to the burning at dusk,' I said. 'At daybreak I'll go.'

She seemed to look past me.

'I think it's best,' I said. 'You are right, that I am immature.'

As I started to cross, past her, to pick up my sword, she said: 'Of course you can't go.'

When I was fourteen I came upon a serf and his woman, coupling behind the sheep-pen below Mynnydd Mawr. I was descending the hillside in leaps, but they had not heard me, and seeing them I stopped, confused, swaying on braced feet; then ducked behind some boulders, in a sort of fear. Not for the purpose of watching, but because there was no fit form for our encounter, no way I could continue past them with an incidental greeting. My face burning with sun, wind, and the rapidity of my descent; breathless from movement; I watched them, from the boulders; and my breathing didn't slacken and my face did not cool.

They were animal. The serf's grunts: the woman's knees slapping his sides. A travesty of man, a representation of the damned. At twenty yards' distance, I yet seemed to smell their heated guts, the pulsing glands. Yet when I tried, once, to roll away and not watch—to stare up at the mountain and settle my mind on a thought of weather and season—I found my ears straining to hear. I was compelled to kneel up and watch

again, my hands bunched below my midriff
against my own rearing excitement. The mon-
strousness of that compulsion exceeded the
mere bestiality of those I watched. At the end,
when they lay collapsed, like winded horses, I
slipped giddily past them in a wide arc, ducking
from boulder to boulder; and so into the woods.
A sort of moaning in my breath—I thought I was
about to be taken very ill, or to run mad. In the
cover of the woods I pressed against the hillside,
shut-eyed, groaning; my legs strained apart, my
hands gripped into fists on the ground under my
forehead; uncomprehendingly I thrust my belly
against the earth, and after a few moments was
sacked by fire. I lay then, laid waste, humiliated,
a shell burning for miles. My undergarment
slimy wet. Wood-insects in my hair. My face in
the palms of my hands.

That seemed near to damnation. My provi-
sional and partial release came when, after a few
days in which my mind was not my own, I managed to tell it to Mansel. That was the hardest
submission I had known, before this day of the
ending of Whiteflower's siege; it was made in the
full fear that when he knew of that monstrous-
ness he would be compelled, for his own sake, to
withdraw his tutelage. I knew how kindly he
would do it, with what discretion and consideration; but I expected—half-expected, I must have
kept some hope as well—the ending of his love.

Instead, he gripped me at the shoulders more
tightly than ever before, and held me against
him, making me talk till there was nothing to say
and what was already spoken seemed, by being
said, and by being so steadily received, less

grave. What few things he said to settle me were much what you might have said; what I remember are not his words but his acceptance, his shrewd eyes imagining my wretchedness, his open face. In the end he touched his bearded lips to my wet cheek; then set me to work greasing harness. He made me sing, as we worked.

The half-hour before I brought myself to speak of this to Mansel was a time cut loose from ordinary time, adrift, unsteady, and so it was before the greater release, there with my lady. Not wretched, not despairing; closer this time to a delighted frenzy which too might cut me adrift. It was, for all the delight, not far from desolation; and, as on the mountainside at fourteen, I had lost for the moment the knowledge of good. The world was unsteady: I looked at the large room, breathing hard, hard, over a water-mill which clattered inside me, over and over. The sunlight still calm on the floor; Christ-on-the-cross; and herself on the couch, leaf-silks against crimson, her own steadiness going, her trembling growing with mine, within the calm room.

I sat down, at her feet, and began to unfasten my boots. There was no doubt now that I would become her man: resisting, I was also impelled and happy. The shivering resolution was what I knew best from combat, but when preparing to fight I would tighten boots, fasten gauntlets, breastplate, helmet—they were all additions to myself. Now it was necessary to free myself from all protections; the addition would be within me. At last I hurried, to strip—I wanted to settle the matter. It was still in some ways fearful. (Look for me in your own memories.) And Whiteflower watched me, quite silent, only unfastening and laying aside her stole.

Finally I knelt by the couch, naked, as if to pray, and waited for her. She still wore, full-length, her blue undergarment; most of her body I still knew only from suggestion, and now that must change.

We were solemn, that moment! Unsmiling she looked at me, her eyes narrowing a little in tension. Then she shifted partly away and freed the garment at the shoulders; standing, she thrust it quickly down her body, stepped out of it and bent, flashingly, to pick it up. I laughed suddenly, softly. She spread the blue garment out on the head of the couch and sat there then, her knees drawn quickly up to her chin: a girl containing herself, but beginning to smile again. And the solemnity passed. The room was cool: we both shivered a little, and were amused. She reached out and lifted my left wrist towards her, and I scrambled up to sit for a moment on one thigh, my legs curled before me. Whiteflower's hair fell over her shoulders, forward to her knees, her breasts parting the pale stream. Her face, when I lifted my eyes, was deeply flushed now, her eyes racing over me. We knelt to each other.

Here, I imagine you saying, I must surely keep silent: it is experience at once too general and too particular. The unease, and the danger of sacrilege, is yours as well as mine. (Well, but you have to come with me, along my story.)

I think it is a matter of belief, and of trust. A matter of where God is, and where—if anywhere—he is not; of whether you believe that he rides in the wind, or only in the calm. And our privacy, in the intense, God-given experience—is that separation from other life? I think it is conjunction.

But to tell is to regret, perhaps; some sadness comes in such telling, by me alone, away from her now a long time. My future is other, quite other. I prepare myself for it by understanding my past: by mourning and celebration. I am sorry if this makes you uneasy: it makes me at peace.

Kneeling, we reached to touch each other; our foreheads stooped to each other's neck, we caressed with the side of the head, as the animals do. Wanting to hurry, and not to hurry; laughing softly, and breaking to draw in breath sharply, in half-snorts, and laughing again. The fear and the solemnity had melted, into sweetness.

A woman shouted, below the window, calling a child. Her loud voice, from the matter-of-fact, was puzzlingly close.

All the sunlit afternoons of my life had passed on the dimension of that shout. This present transcendence, close and ordinary, had been that of others.

My lady lifted my hands away from her breasts, placed them herself back at my sides; and brought her own hands, softly, to my penis. I watched, we both watched, as it trembled, straighter in the lined fingertips of her two hands: red, unearthly, independent of me. She slid the thin skin a little backwards and forwards, over its hardness. Then, breathless in a wincing smile, I took her hands away; pressed her back. Watching her eyes mostly, I touched in turn her hips, their inward slope; ran the backs of my fingers feathery again and again up the smoothness inside her thighs, to the hair—and away again, delaying. When I looked down between her grey, opening hips I was dizzy, with the simple delight. Slowly, all the time laughing back the tearing hurry inside myself, I hooked my hands beneath her knees, and tipped her, very slowly, backwards, smiling at her smiling, drawing her legs from underneath and spreading them. Thinking of the morning field, of Gagreth and Saglar and the evening pyre to come, I sank my face to her breasts, my hands sliding up her legs to the hot corner, centre of her, moist to my fingers.

The continual lightness which flurried, half-laughter, between us was partly, perhaps, memory of what till now we had been to each other—what we still were to the world. The very young and serious hero: the restrained, faintly ironic lady. We could be amused at the width between ourselves and those lesser selves. And we laughed because we had given up protections, we were open to each other.

Also, one laughs with incredulity. Whiteflower's fingers travelled in my hair, and tightened, then reached down my cheek, drawing my face towards her. I lifted myself on my elbow, kissed her lips, her temple; then touched and closed again my hand upon her right breast; and Whiteflower tipped her head abruptly backwards, into her own poured hair on the blazing pillow, till I saw only her pale throat and opened lips. Lifting myself further I kissed both breasts, to the sound of a lost, girl's laughter from her thrown-back head. Eventually, laying her head on one side on the bright cushion, she looked at me again, eyes wide, her lips quivering, her nostrils fluttering and hardening—fragility and tenderness there, and in myself a fast simplicity of passion. I lost my mouth in her open lips, my hands in her hair, moulding the shining hairs against her heated throat and white shoulders.

For a moment we ceased to move; as if we had both drawn back breath and, with that, the day had stopped, the sun stood still. I thought, only distantly now, of the life below and around us, the mild afternoon, the sublunary men and women to whom the two of us, separated, would later return; for the present my ears were full of the beat of blood, and the chance sibilances of my lady's strong breathing. Then she pressed me gently back, half-up from her; tipped her head forward and widened her legs again, knocking her left knee under me, bringing me to the centre of her. With her fingers she drew me into her body.

Like wafer upon the tongue, at the First Communion: that was a physical sensation of abstract importance, so crucial in my beliefs that its physical nature seemed—even the dry wafer— a little gross. Then, the blood on my lips. For a time I resisted the physical symbolism of the spiritual mystery, and was partly alarmed, to have it on my tongue. Now, taken in to sweetness, I was for a few breaths startled in the mind, my reason blowing away down a plunging valley; and for a little while I couldn't yield and couldn't link. Gasping, murmuring across her strained face as she turned in spite of herself away from me, teeth biting down her lower lip, I knew, and had to accept, that she remembered in those first moments her husband; just as I also knew

myself to be remembering the code, and leaving
some aspects of that behind (or, I would now
rather say, re-interpreting them). Mansel's love,
and my mother: I left them behind me on a thin
road up which I rode loudly, pounding; behind
me the dust-clouds, ahead the peaks—wind-
chill, sun-burst. Now I was working something
out, for her, for my lady Whiteflower, my love-
lady, something between us and of us—again, I
am sorry if it is simple and familiar, but it was
not familiar to me then, it was a discovery. . . . Of
this indeed one can't speak, it is outside words.

To finish what I began, I use them. There was
a last corner turned, spurring suddenly
upwards; then, in maroon incandescence behind
my clenched eyes, I was fully loosened, and
poured into her. Generosity, of nature beyond
myself, beyond us both. And Whiteflower thrown
there with me, entirely with me, in rainbow
spray, sea-foam, dragged on the roaring beach;
and moving a little longer, heavily, against me.
Generosity. Generosity beyond our power; falling
gradually still. We lay, settling, open and blessed;
settling to peace, in the generous world.

With the opening of my gland I felt I had
opened a direct way to God. Mock me not. A
direct way to God, opened at the centre of us,
weak, given, still open. The wind blew now into
us as well as out of us. Through our bodies had
passed, and now, while the passage lay still
open, returned, life of the world: the unbroken
energy and calm at the heart of things. I was finished with separations. I was merged, and my
lady with me, with the dust of the room, the
roughness of wood, and the now-restored noises

of the afternoon. There was no gap. We were part of the processes of God.

I remember I let my hand trail to the floor. My fingernails, faintly, scraped the uneven rushes. A few inches from my hand the sunlight edged, by the minutes of our lying still there, around the room. In my nostrils was the smell of our sweat. I thought: I have not, before, so known I am alive.

3

For nearly two years I have been telling the same story: the true story. More briefly than here, for now I'm telling it to myself as well as to you, in a hope of understanding. But in house after house, by camp fires, in place after place where Arthur is said to have been, but is no longer, I tell what happened to me. My story goes round to meet me now, I've started a legend indeed, though it holds no giants. Sometimes now in the course of my narrative a child or an old woman—someone who hasn't learnt courtesy, or has forgotten it—breaks out with a relaxed cry, and tells me to swallow my story, they heard the same from a Welsh minstrel a month ago. The adults then are embarrassed, courteous, they ask me to continue; but their eyes too puzzle into me, seeing me as a fantasist, a disturbed youth persuading himself he has lived a legend. Some tell me frankly they do not believe in Arthur. Others, however, are positive about his goodness and his whereabouts.

It becomes penance, to tell my story; or a payment in kind for a widow's hospitality, or a place by the hall fire of a large house. Yet I would always tell it, in the hope of guidance.

Usually I keep it short. I tell them of my uncertain fatherhood, in the village where the mountains fall away towards the coastal strip, where, from a high ridge in clear weather, I could look to both northern and western seas. Most of my audiences have never seen a sea; they respect my account because they have heard many similar, and similarly circumstantial, from other travellers. I doubt, too, whether when I speak of mountains they picture much more than the scrub-covered easy hills they know: so a certain savagery in my upbringing may not, then, communicate itself entirely. But they recognize from their own experience the goodness—believable and unlegendary goodness—of the man Mansel, who without marrying my mother befriended her and made me his pupil for everything he knew in the world. And they respect my love of my mother, about which I can't speak fluently.

Of Mansel's murder I tell them, the simple fact; and of my departure two months later, alone. Sometimes when women hear this they protest, as if my own mother were there in the room. When, as is frequent, my lodging in a settlement is with a widow or an abandoned mother, there are difficult silences at this point. Sometimes their own sons are abroad as I am; are with Arthur or searching for him, or have died with him.

In the morning of the day I leave, they often try to persuade me to return home.

Then it is the traveller's sequence, which must bear some kinship to many they hear, from many who pass through. I tell them only of the remote abbey, in a valley of thorns and swamp, where I rested three weeks and where the abbot gave me his advice: to be restrained, to accept experience but not to beat it out of the bushes, to keep my cautious silence with strangers. And of my lady Whiteflower, whose house I freed from the besiegers and with whom I passed the entire winter that followed: Whiteflower whom I loved and to whom, if God allows, I hope at last to return.

And I tell them of Henged, the suffering lord, as I shall tell you. His placidity in the afternoon light, knee-deep in a glittering river, spearing a large trout from above, and lifting it streaming from the water towards me. His fearlessness of a stranger, and freedom from suspicion; his delicately concealed hope. The ride to his castle, in the soft afternoon, watched from the high platform. The procession, at the evening feast, shouting, ceremony. His face haunts. Kindness. Suffering. Shouts, dependence; he is the ageing father. And I am silent, as I have been advised.

The spear pours blood; the girl holds the cup; her eyes watch the running blood. Beating waves of pain, in the magic hall. The night, and the empty morning.

The mists begin here—the magic I was not seeking, and did not recognize. From here I'm less surely my own.

Again and again I stoop through, pressing back the door sharply, and step out, on to the platform. The light dazzles a little, but there is no danger: the platform too is deserted. The blade-edge of the parapet's shadow runs down the middle of the boardwalk; half the bleached oak dry in the sunlight, dustgrains glittering; half in the green dark-light of the wall. There is nowhere that a man might be concealed.

I could draw all of it, every jut and hollow, from memory.

There is no haze: a spring rawness of light. Hills on the horizon twenty miles distant are clear, slate-blue; and between it is an intricate coloured landscape, palpitating in the heat-shimmer. It is a brilliant light, and a sane land-scape; but the house's life is magicked. I open my lips, to make a last shout, and then don't bother to stir my throat. There is no listener.

I tap one spur, without purpose, against the parapet. The small scrape and ringing begin to echo, then the vast sky takes them. But the stone is real enough; ordinary, spring-sun-lit. I am reluctant to leave.

Telling of this is as hard as telling of making love, and the difference is that this must be told, in public, to everyone. When it's over, they offer little in the way of interpretation. They have heard, sometimes, the outline before; the legend seems to have travelled so well, ahead of me, that I wonder occasionally if it has not hap-pened to others, on previous times. They respect me, but mark me off with slightly more dis-tance—as if the magic is a little within me; or is all mine, my delusion.

I don't fear that. I don't doubt my own sani-ty—I would say, normality, except that I recog-nize that my life is unusual. I am sane enough; my lady Whiteflower would say that I am pre-dictably straightforward. But now I think I'm

changing, and not from my own will. God who
made me so hard in my own identity is now
breaking me down, softly; I'm not my own, in the
same way. I began to change—it began to be *necessary* for me to change—that morning on the
sunlit platform above the fisher-lord's empty
house. In the sane air and the raw light: my spur
tapping, purposeless, against the stone parapet:
the small brief echo.

I tell it as it was—and more fully here. And in the
first year, away from home, the year of newly-
hardened identity, it was sharp, vivid to grasp: I
had no doubt about those encounters. At the
start it was clearly heroic. In one day, after only
a week at Whiteflower's house, I killed or helped
to kill Gagreth and eleven of his raiders, became
my lady's lover, and burnt, at dusk, the corpses
of my enemies. Even then, maybe, it was reli-
gious too: God in the cool room-air, as
Whiteflower and I lay, sometimes sleeping, sometimes waking, through the afternoon.

Whiteflower's man of God, however, was a
drunkard.

At first his difficulty, at dusk that day, in
crossing the tussock ground to the pyre, assist-
ed by the boy who was his personal servant and
also, I discovered later, his son, seemed mainly a
matter of age and gripped joints. And his half-
coherent reading might be blamed on the uneven
torchlight. He plucked with his hand at the shadows till the nearest torch-holder came so near
that the tallow fell, unnoticed, on his sleeve. But
they were words he should have known by heart,
as the chaplain of the house; and once when, as

if suddenly terrified, bewildered, he lifted his
head and his eyelids to stare at the dark mass of
the pyre, and at the ring of us there, lit by the
stinking and hissing torches, I caught the man's
eyes and saw their drugged confusion.

A man supposed to be the master of darkness, the settler of death; dragged out in a frosty
dusk to the beginning of a night he simply
feared, to speak words he had ceased to understand. The looming pile of dead, beginning their
long night of death, pressed the words back at
his lips. He was not drunk because this was a
day of victory (as some of the men now unconscious in the house had made themselves
drunk), nor as the one who here at the ceremony
vomited where he stood, confronting the corpses,
and then stood swaying and coughing through
the mumbled words. The chaplain was drunk, I
saw, because he was drunk every day at this
time; at the approach of night.

It would have been easier not to have called
him out: that was what my lady had advised. But
he was the man of God, drunk or sober; and it
was necessary that he should speak God's words
over the dead. I might echo them silently, clearly, on my own lips as I listened; but on my lips
they could be only a prayer, not a ceremony.

When I burnt my friend, it was with prayers
only. The holy man had died himself, peacefully,
three weeks earlier, and we had no other. We
gave Mansel to fire, like this: myself and my
mother and a few villagers grouped in the afternoon dusk of winter, in an interval between
showers. Grey on-rolling skies, the driving westerly clouds furred in the dusk, tawny in the

brand-light; and the few mourners loaded with their heaviest skins and furs, against the gusting wind. We had built Mansel's pyre on the slope above his own hut, slightly in the lee of the rising ridge—in the full wind the fire would not have taken at all. Burial was not our custom: in the valley the land is too wet, on the hills too bald and hard and, at that season, frozen land under frozen snow. In gauntlets and fur hats and tied skins we carried the body of Mansel up to the trodden area and the pyre, and started the fire with cow-fat and hay from the centre of the stack. The flames flared wildly in the wind, sometimes horizontally for half a minute, not reaching his body at all. As the wind blew night over us, and cast a few slashes of sleet in our faces, I became frightened that we would be unable to burn him: that a smoked unconsumed body must be abandoned there or lugged grotesquely down the hill to the hut again. Yet it was no fault of mine or ours, that we hadn't the holy man for the ceremony.

I was weeping, in the sleet and wind.

But over my enemies, Whiteflower's enemies, the words were duly spoken, even if drunkenly. I whispered them also myself. and watched the other men's faces. There were only nine in all; the rest were asleep or incapable. These looked weary, or bitter. The sky was clear, the night tightening into frost.

Death pushed them back, from their confidence—even the deaths of their enemies. It was not the chaplain only who was unused to being abroad in darkness. They were afraid of the night, and made me share the uneasiness.

When the torches went into the pyre, the gloom cramped in upon us for a few moments. From the far side of our ring I heard a grown man's murmuring gasp. Then the dry wood caught, quickly. Several men stepped back a little, at the leaping energy of fire. It took so easily. I watched with narrowed eyes, remembering how I had almost despaired, at Mansel's funeral. It was a brief panic—five minutes, or ten— but it was the nearest in my life I had been, at that time, to despair. It was Mansel's advice I needed, Mansel's steadying. Mansel I was trying to burn.

When Mansel spoke finally, in my mind, it was with a lean patience: I must leave it to God, having done what I could myself. Soon after that the fire began to fasten upon the body. Heat reaching our faces, while our limbs and feet were chilled.

Here too, in the still night, warmth came to us. A noisy light began to fan across the men's figures, enlarging them: a hand instinctively restless on a dagger hilt, a shimmer from greased boots, perhaps Gagreth's own; the eyes of the old one-armed man Waldin firmly closed. Dazzled, or reverent? The fire gathered excitement, like hounds at a kill; its rapid brightness thickened the night over our heads and at our backs, made an end of dusk. The men shifted, glancing at each other, relaxing a little, as the wood gabbled of its own consuming. Some watched as the flames touched and closed upon the corpses; others looked at each other, at my eyes, at the base of the fire. To the side of my vision I saw the old chaplain move away. The boy

conducting him had no torch, but it was not so
far back to the house.

I forced myself to observe the fire, as it
destroyed the bodies.

A man's head, at the end of the pyre near me,
was haloed in flame as the hair and beard burnt,
and then continued to glow red, like peat; and
the skin of the face tightened and altered; fire-
years ageing it, breaking it down, to the skull. I
couldn't watch for long.

But better than the wolves. The smells were
foul, but would pass as the bodies passed. The
fire simplified and cleaned. In the morning there
would be only the clean charred smell. Already,
too, though it resembled suffering it was nothing
of the kind. When the fire reached Mansel's features, I remember, I saw it with relief, and
thanks. Nothing so steadily showed his death, so
acknowledged and fulfilled it, as this: that what
would have been, in the living man whatever his
courage, unbearable pain, was here received as a
sacrament. It was time for his frozen flesh to
melt, and yield.

We didn't speak or sing, as we watched
Mansel burn. There was only the noise of the
wind and the flaming pyre, snarling suddenly in
a gust, slackening then to lick and glow; and
later the hiss of wet snowflakes in the flames. At
last, whitened ourselves with snow on head and
shoulders and in all the drift-crannies of our
clothing, we left him, to kick our way downhill;
the snow, lit by torchlight, flaring sideways at us
and the torches themselves sick, half-out. I
crouched aside once, my back hunched against
the thicker and thicker snow, and sheltered my

eyes with my gauntlet, to peer up again at
Mansel's pyre: the flames were struggling on,
seen through a bustling mist of snowflakes, and
lighting the hillside's fresh whiteness. The elements were taking him quickly away from us
now, across a gaping distance.

Perhaps I supply it in memory, but I don't believe
so. As I watched the flames finishing Gagreth
and his raiders, a face not only Mansel's
repeatedly brightened and faded on the back of
my brain. Not a face out of life that I knew, but a
face from emblem, vision, or dream: interlaid
there with the features of my enemies and the
features of my friend, but not the same as either;
and not in death but in pain. I thought of pain as
I saw those heads shrivel and seethe, of pain
beyond bearing; but I knew they were not in fact
in pain, yet through the fire I saw, coming and
going, the emblem-face, in pain. A man parted
from himself by pain not death; aged by pain
though not old; decades invading his face within
moments; the flesh breaking down. I know more,
of course, now; but I want to tell it as it was. I
saw the face through the fire, but it was not a
face in the fire, it was not burning, and it was not
assuaged by death.

For a breath or two, tired by the extremity of
the day gone past, I imagined it was Christ, calling to me, and my skin shrank. I must take holy
advice. Then I thought of the chaplain, wryly.

One of the cross-pieces of the fire slipped and
fell, tipping the weight of corpses unevenly sideways, and dipping into the centre of the flames.
The fire hastened up the new line, and its blaze

seemed to strengthen. Perhaps because of this, of something loosened suddenly in the atmosphere, a young man began to sing.

He had been drinking since morning, his hard-boned face glistened with sweat though the night was freezing; and he sang, suddenly loud, what was evidently a communal victory song, though I didn't recognize it. The others joined in quickly, and closed up together, away from me, at the far end of the pyre. It meant nothing hostile to me; there were too few of them to make a joined ring about the fire, and the song urged them together. I stayed at my end, seeing now their heads through the flames, a shouting group; and between us, in my tired brain, came Mansel, Gagreth, the emblem-face, flashing with the crude song. Great lurching stresses carried the song; those with swords or staves jabbed them upwards, the tips flying into darkness, and in spite of their weary half-drunkenness the rhythm hardened steadily as they sang. Song and words were stripped down to yelled voice-blows on the night. It was like flogging the night, flogging the travelling souls.

I turned, into darkness, and set off alone for the house. I had no light with me, but at first the rough land bulked into reddish-lit mounds and black shadows, and I could choose a way quickly. Later I stumbled, beginning to make only a few slow steps at a time. There was no hurry: I was willing to linger, between the fire and the house. Several times I stopped still, letting the windless air grip about me.

Tonight, and the nights to come, I would sleep in Whiteflower's bed. Not making love always, or only; but sleeping the night, falling asleep in sharing, and waking in it.

Trying to think of this, there were blank places in my mind, and some instinctive oppositions.

The time of preparing for sleep, and waiting for sleep, had always been my own, only mine, whether it was in a separate part of a house or in the corner of a communal hall. For my adolescent life, it was the base, from which I went out to the day. The evening and morning prayer: images in the mind before sleep: the body curled warmly and defensively on itself.

To sleep with my lady would be good, an accession to manhood; but it seemed to me that the base would still be in myself and God. I would still want to arrange myself, and be private, before going out to the night as to the day.

I put this now more clearly than it worked in my heart that evening. Then it was confusion, oppositions and blank places, which I couldn't clarify. I remember (it flushes my face to remember) wondering whether I would kneel and pray, as always before sleep, with my lady there in the chamber. And then what? Close a mental door on God, and make love?

God had been with us and generous with us, in the afternoon.

Standing there in the night I did see that I was still partly a boy. Some of the more raw and tense moments of our afternoon had marked that. As a man I would come to be easier with her, less insistent. It was better to see where I hadn't yet grown, and accept that. I wouldn't try to trick myself in my mind.

I should have brought with me a brand from the fire. Behind me the singing had stopped, but the men were still grouped together, talking—a blur of laughter rose occasionally. The pyre lit them and was the only light, a red cut of existence on a black field of nothing. We were all a little alarmed by the night.

I looked over my head. The sky was still a milder darkness than the earth, and there were many stars, but only a slit of moon. I set out again, coming soon to the low, wet area, of mud and marsh. Testing each footstep, I made it a game for myself, to cross dry-footed and be always in balance. The chaplain and the boy must have had an awkward return.

When the porter admitted me, back at the house, he worked his mouth a little, perhaps surprised to see me alone. He smiled at me, and took my wrist for a moment. An old crippled man of some dignity, looking up with pale clear eyes.

'Left them, young one, have you?'

'Yes, father.'

He kept his clutch on my wrist, with his bony fingers. His smile was shrewd and somehow delighted.

I asked him: 'Did the chaplain get back?'

'Not long since.' He nodded, closing his eyes a moment. 'And to bed, I should hope.'

I laughed. 'He's been celebrating, as much as anyone.'

'Ah.' The old man's cheekbones seemed to lift as he grinned. 'You and me, boy,' he patted my wrist, 'we're the only ones left sober in the house. You and me and a few of the women.'

'Perhaps I'll drink now, a little,' I said.

I glanced towards the hall opening. The women were singing in there; better singing than that of the men at the pyre, but still a thick sound which made me uneasy. I looked at the porter again. 'I wanted to see the dead dealt with, first.'

He nodded again, not taking his narrowed eyes off me.

'Drink little, young one,' he said. 'My lady waits for you.'

I looked towards the hall again, and felt my face filling with blood.

'Is she in there?' I said.

'Ah no!' He laughed gently. 'In her chamber, my lord.'

I met his eyes. 'Then I must go to see her.'

'Sure you must.' He laughed softly, his cheek-bones pressing at his eyes. 'Surely you must.' He opened his hand and lifted it to my shoulder, in a frail slap. 'You, young one, it's the greatest day of your life, ain't it? But you're modest like a knight. Well enough. That's a hero.'

I trusted him not to mock me; the smile in his eyes was kind. I said, whispering, glancing aside in case anyone approached: 'You shouldn't expect too much of me.'

He waited, nodding, watching my face.

'I want to be a hero, father; and today the luck was all mine. But, you know well enough, I'm young, I can easily be a fool. . . . And just now, I'm tired.'

I smiled, and began to move away. His hand tried to keep my arm.

'Look in on the women for one cup of wine, my lord. If you don't they'll all be unsatisfied.'

He grinned. I flushed, and said, laughing, 'But what about my lady?'

'Ah, she'll wait a while. Just go in and smile at the others a little, then we'll all have some peace.'

Then, as I moved away towards the hall, he lifted his voice, calling me back.

'My lord.' He beckoned me, and continued flapping his hand towards himself, as if to whisper a confidence. I stooped my head to him. He placed both his hands on my shoulders and laid his cheek clumsily against mine, first one side, then the other. His hands gripped my shoulders hard, quivering. His breath smelt as if he had not long to live.

'God be with you, young one,' he whispered. 'You saved us.'

As I approached the hall threshold, while I was still out of sight in the dark archway, the women's noise inside surged suddenly into laughter: it fell back momentarily, then reared up again. Something was there which they were all laughing at, together.

I leant back from the doorpost: tired, reluctant to face them. From his nook the porter was watching. I smiled slightly back at him, lifting my shoulders. Then I dipped my head round the doorway, to look in.

Down the centre of the candle-lit hall a woman was walking away from me: one of the oldest and fattest of the women, strutting away, and carrying—her thick arm crooked in a parody of the readiness position—my spear. Behind her,

on the floor, making gargoyle grimaces of suffering, was sprawled on her back a younger, but
heavy and already moustached woman. The
irregular lines of women either side didn't know
which to watch, which was the funnier.

They appeared to have been drinking almost
as much as the men. One red-haired girl, near
the doorway, my own age or less, was asleep, or
unconscious at least, in the arms of an older
woman, perhaps her mother. Her face was dust-
white, glistening. Several others looked
reduced, slack-faced, their brains clotted by the
wine. Laughter knocked them all around at present, blew them and bent them and lifted their
hands and heads; they were like threshing trees
in wind.

'You saved us.' I had saved them.

What the laughter said was, that they had
been very frightened. By this time, if Gagreth had
swept into the house as he had expected, the
young redhead would have been raped, perhaps
then stripped and whipped to dance, perhaps
killed. The same for many of the others. The children would have been murdered, perhaps violated first.

They had hardly hoped to be here now,
laughing.

Why they were parodying me, I didn't understand. I was more worried than angered by it.
But it seemed a matter of honour to go and meet
the parody, and take if necessary the laughter on
to myself.

The old woman carrying the spear turned, as
she reached the end of the room—a lurching
swing. She was laughing herself, her face

streaming and red. Her body was slack, spread;
mother of ten, maybe. Not all that old, after all,
when I looked again. And it wasn't a witch's face:
it was thickly-fleshed, sweating, contorted in
laughter; a whore's face perhaps, well outside the
code, but human enough.

Swaying there at the end of the room, she
made lumbering curtseys to her audience either
side of her. Then she brought the spear down in
front of her, and swung her big hips astride it.

The women shrieked as if at a disaster: hands
pressed to eyes, heads and throats thrown back.

The parody-Percival lifted the spearhead at an
angle, and fondled the tip, at the same time wig-
gling her hips around the shaft.

The laughter seemed to go almost beyond
retrieve.

At its height, I stepped slowly into the hall. I
was very tired, and trembling: it was the third
ordeal of the day, and the most bewildering. My
whole face and neck must be scarlet, absurd
with the flush: but in the candlelight and their
hysteria they might scarcely see that.

So I stood, at the end of the central aisle,
above the parody-victim, and waited until everyone in the hall knew I was there. They grew quiet
more quickly than I had expected, though some
of the more hysterical continued with choked
sobbing and giggling. While I waited, I tried to
keep on my lips a slight smile. They meant no
harm. I looked slowly round their faces. Blinking
rather often, the backs of my knees shaking, I
still tried to meet their eyes, and keep up that
small smile. They need mean no contempt, by
the parody. I'd seen other parodies—of the Green

Man or of Christ, or simply children's parodies of
their fathers—which grew from reverence, not
contempt. I saw no hostility in their eyes; they
were dazed, embarrassed; and they knew I had
saved them.

I walked up the aisle then, in near-silence, as
if in a ceremony, and smiled at my parody-self.
She had stepped back from the spear, and held
it now upright at her side; and she met my look
with her head jutted a little, a bit defiant. Maybe
I had saved her, the look seemed to say, but to
her I was still a boy. She was a grandmother,
probably. She had seen heroes come and go.

I reached for the spear with my left hand,
gripped it and, leaning to her, kissed her lightly
on both her cheeks. My lips met hair there, my
nostrils met a rancidness of sweat and wine.
Then as I stood back from her she broke into a
loud laugh, and slapped me on the shoulder; and
the room filled up again with noise, and relief.

Holding the spear, I turned: I lifted it high,
raising my other hand too. When they were quiet
again I said:

'I am told that before going to bed—'

Two shrieks of laughter, which started the
others off again, briefly.

I dipped my head a moment, then lifted it and
said, more loudly:

'Before going to bed I am to drink a cup of
wine with you.'

A murmur of agreement: they nodded and
began chattering, smiling at me, talking in each
other's ears. Several women raised their own
cups loosely towards me, but I held back, in the
middle of the hall. They would offer me more for-

mally a victor's cup. I saw the huddle in the corner, the big woman whom I had kissed gesticu-
lating to a young girl, making some explanation.

I turned, and walked back away from them, to
the end of the hall near the doorway; then swung
round to stand looking down the aisle, waiting.

The big woman lifted both her arms suddenly, facing the room. Dark sweat-patches under
her shoulders. She jabbered quickly at the qui-
etening women, words I couldn't follow. Much of
their dialect passed me by, in those first days.
But the women began, then, to sing. Beginning
hesitantly, then singing more firmly, though not
loud. They had become once more gentle and
feminine, for my benefit. I half-closed my eyes,
listening; I still heard in my head remnants of
their raucous laughter, a few moments earlier.

The song was a wandering movement around
three or four notes. I didn't know it, but the mode
could be recognized. It was a love-song, a pledge-
song, the lover dedicating himself.

From the far end, the young girl began to
walk, alone, towards me. She carried a silver
cup, heavily ornamented, and it was brimming
with wine. The cup I had seen before, where it
stood in a recess at that end of the hall: it must
be the ceremony-cup of Whiteflower's husband.
As the girl passed from the influence of one can-
dle-cluster to another, the mouldings of the silver
shone and faded, and changed continually in the
relief. Set around the base of the cup were jewels, concentrating the energy of the light.

She was about fourteen. My heart tightened
suddenly with pity for her, among the older
women's grossness. Shadows marked where her

small breasts rose against her clothing; shadows were deep between her thin shoulders and her collarbones. I could watch her face as she approached, because it was held full to me though her eyes were always cast down upon the brimming cup. Her lips were moving; she was whispering the song herself. Her face was ungrown, hollowed but smooth; cheekbones and the lower curves of the face made a symmetry directed downwards, tapering towards the cup, held at breast-height in her trembling hands.

As she reached me and stopped, the singing warmed into a repeated refrain. Behind her I glimpsed the intent, jealous watchers.

The girl lifted her eyes and set back her shoulders, as if deciding something firmly—nervous, but committed, and smiling to me. I had passed the spear to my left hand; now I lifted my right, to take the cup; but she shook her head, withdrawing it slightly. Then she reached with her own right hand towards the spear, bringing it down towards her, until she could touch the tip. Then, still holding the cup more or less steadily in her left hand, she dipped her right hand in the wine and returned it to the spearhead, wetting it with her fingers. And the same again and again, till the wine dripped from the spear to the floor and a little ran down the shaft and over my hand.

Through mists, the parody seen before the real. I was already marked, not knowing it. I watched her watching the wine, a stream on the spearhead. The singing had stopped. Rustlings, murmured breath, were around us.

The girl lifted her hand to her own lips, licking the wine from her fingers, and passed the cup to me, smiling again, bright-eyed now. I held it a moment, looking past her to the watching faces and secretly, through parted lips, filling my lungs with air; then shut my eyes and lifted the cup and drank.

4

A round Christmas-time it rained heavily, day after day. For several weeks there was no frost, and little sunshine; but almost unceasing westerly wind, whipping more and more rain against the buildings and the flooded land. In the hall of Whiteflower's house, and in the kitchen, there were always people or their clothing in front of the big fires, drying out, with a heavy animal steaming. In Whiteflower's own chamber, rain hissed in the fire, when the wind blew a certain way, and made puddles on the floor beneath the windows. In many places the roof leaked, and above one gallery it collapsed, on a foul afternoon two days before Christmas: a day still dusky at noon, with thick rain making grey invisibility at twenty yards.

The men dropped their heads and mumbled, when it was a question of going up to mend it. I had to go up myself, with one old man who had helped to make the roof years before, and who had no fear. We retrieved the slumped thatch and lashed a fresh wooden support beneath it. The exposed height did trouble me—the gale seemed likely to pull a whole half-roof away, and us two with it, and throw us into the flooded ditch out-

side the walls. If we hadn't made the repair, half
the roof might in fact have been torn away, within the next few hours. I was soaked to the skin in
a few minutes, my fingers—scratched in dragging back the thatch—whitening with cold but
running with a mixture of blood and rain. The
old man seemed somehow to keep drier: an old
toad, squatting without security there on the
angled roof, knotting the reed-rope. When a vio-
lent swash of wind and water hit him, he lifted
his left hand and tugged a little at his hood, leaning forward slightly further into the wind; but
otherwise seemed not to notice.

Afterwards I huddled in front of my lady's fire,
rubbed by her, then heaped with her furs. The
furs excited me; soon I was gripping her wrists,
coughing with laughter, pulling her into the fireplace with me, and we made love, in a long, teas-
ing, familiar way, having time to fill. The fire
burned our cheeks, our legs, our arms, as the
furs slipped away from us; and repeatedly we
rolled over and pulled them around us again, to
stay in the fire's heat without roasting.

It grew quickly dark, so that the heat was the
light too: glinting flashes of vision in a mostly
shut-eyed, touch-smothered life. All the time, the
wind and rain flailed on outside. The bell in the
nearby belfry creaked constantly and in the
gusts the clapper knocked faintly against the
bell, as if spilling—like a harbour wall at spring
tide—a force it couldn't entirely hold.

That was a good hour or two in a generally
depressed time. On the roof, though frightened,
and physically miserable, I had at least found
myself in action, after a series of swamped days

in which I had hardly been out of the building. For some time the most energetic activity I'd found had been wrestling on straw with the better wrestlers among the men of the house: the three best were heavier and more skilful than I, and could always put me down. I continued to tackle them, for the experience and the exercise; but it would have helped my spirits if I could have won occasionally.

And Whiteflower, now, lived mostly as if part of her was withdrawn. I think she was not discontented, but, through all the grey weather, she was subdued, folded in on herself; if not saddened, still somehow diminished. The laughing excitement that afternoon in the fireplace was rare. Most of the day she kept in her chamber, showing herself less often to the people, sometimes going only to chapel. The authority in the house was more and more mine. That was, she said, how she wished it; it was more natural. I knew everyone now by name, what they did and what one could expect of them.

For the midnight Mass of the Nativity I gathered every man and woman, and the older children, into the small chapel. Only a few of us were able to follow the words; most of the people, shifting awkwardly in the darkness behind us, were merely quiet, their thoughts perhaps a blur between fear and sentiment. I thought, repeatedly, of my mother, at the communal ceremony in our village; amongst the others but, as she knelt, alone. We had all left her. Certainly she would be thinking of me, at that same time. The birth of Christ was set back a little from us, because of our own separation.

I prayed for her, as I still do, every morning and
night, for longer and with more care than I
prayed for myself or Whiteflower or anyone else I
then knew. Usually I prayed in the chapel;
always alone, except for the presence of a
kitchen-girl I sometimes saw when I rose at
dawn. The first time I came upon her she was
kneeling alone, at the side of the chapel, as if the
central place were only for those who used it in
processions. When she heard me she swung her
head loose-haired over her shoulder, interrupting
her prayer, and began to flounder to her feet. I
had to gesture sharply, and hold her with my
eyes to show that I meant it, before she would
return to her kneeling; and then, I guessed, she
cut her prayers short. After that I took to opening the big door as quietly as possible, and on
several mornings she wasn't aware of me until
she got up to leave. Still she would not enter if I
were there before her. At night I saw no one.

In the early days, when alone anywhere in the
place, I was forever on guard, following the quietly impassioned drilling of my tutor Mansel, who
had himself at last been surprised despicably.
Later I came to trust the house and its people; its
darkness too—I would slip into the chapel without light, and step slowly down the short aisle in
blackness perfect but for the three high windows
and their faint moderation by stars or moon. On
the less dark nights my eyes quickly discovered
things—picked out the unlit candles on the altar,
and the cross itself.

This silence—solitude—was still vital to me: a
base ground from which I went out to life. I had,
I think, a fair understanding of myself in those

days—better, perhaps, than now, in my altered quest—and I certainly understood that one didn't grow up totally and suddenly. The beard was still slow to come. I was not too often hurt or impatient at this. I had been a child, and would always be the child of God. To my mother I had been son and half-husband; I was still her son and prayed that I could be still, through intercession, her protector. None of this could I naturally share with my lady.

I could, though, pray in her presence if I wished. There was an understanding, that is, of our separate privacies; and I could be in her company and not feel my mind invaded. I think that's important for lovers. After the midnight Christmas service I prayed briefly, in her chamber, kneeling with my elbows on the window-niche, holding bunched in my fingers the cross from around my neck, the cross my mother had given me. Outside it was raining lightly again, cold moistness drifting in at me.

Behind me, Whiteflower was undressing. She moved between me and the twin candlestick, which was at the bed's side; and when my eyes opened at the end of my prayer I saw the heavy fanning shadows, moving large on the wall. I opened my hand on the small silver cross, and looked at it, remembering being given it. Then I slipped it down the front of my tunic, and stood up, turning to her.

As she found me watching her, Whiteflower dropped her hands and smiled a little, meeting my eyes.

'Christmas prayers,' she said quietly.

Then she turned a little away from me, unclasping her undergarment, and adding: 'She'll be praying for you too, at this time.'

'Yes, if all is well with her.'

I began to undress.

'She has more cause to fear for your safety, than you for hers.'

'There are few enough perils here.'

'Since Gagreth. But she can't know that.'

'If she could only see, how I've become domestic.'

She laughed a little.

I stepped quickly to join her in the bed, and pinched out the candles. We lay suddenly side by side in blackness, my hand lifting to find her shoulder, hers reaching more warmly across my body. I lay on my back and spoke upwards into the black room.

'She'd be impressed, I think. And she'd treat you as a daughter. With a great wealth of sentiment.'

I tried to laugh again. Suddenly I desolately missed my mother; I felt speared by sadness.

"More likely she'd be jealous.' Whiteflower's half-whisper had hardened a little. She rubbed her knuckles, familiarly, at the place where my breastbone and collarbones meet, then opened her hand upward, cupping my jaw—as if to stop me saying more.

I didn't try to speak more; I lay, tightening myself a little against her kindness, which might confuse itself in my heart with the sudden home-sick child's longing. I opened my eyes and made them roam, wide, about the invisible ceiling—as

if wine had made the room begin to fold away
from me. If I shut my eyes I might weep.

Whiteflower's hand moved slowly over my
neck and shoulder.

'She doesn't want you to be a knight,' she said.

I rolled my head aside, towards her. I couldn't
see her, but her breath was within inches of me.
(Now I am sick at heart for *that*. I have ridden
away, in my life, from so much kindness.) Eventually I murmured, 'With a part of her, I think
she does want it. She would be proud. With part
of themselves, most mothers would like—I think—
to be a hero's mother. But the rest of them
speaks against it. Many knights die before their
mothers. And most are separated from them.'

'But yours didn't try to keep you.'

I breathed in. 'She understands the code. And
God, maybe, steadied her heart. When I pray, I
pray that he continues to do that.'

During the New Year feast, snow began to fall,
after a drier and colder day. A servant mentioned
it as he refilled our cups, and others around the
table nodded at each other as they heard of it:
almost relieved, it seemed, that the winter was
finally hardening. Lifting the filled cup to my lips,
in the centre of the relaxed energy of the room,
the merriment feast, I saw suddenly in my brain
Mansel's face, its life aching out, snow steadily
covering it. His abandoned body at the mountain pass.

Deliberately, as I lowered my cup, I laughed
aloud, brazening out the memory; I leaned
across to the younger Ewan and asked him
whether he knew the story about the twins who

became bishop and rustler. I forced myself into
the story. Later there was singing, and some
heavy dancing in which my lady and I were oblig-
ed to lead.

At one point in the long confused hours, I
stepped outside into the house-yard to make
water, and found already a half-inch of soft snow
there. The big flakes, freed there from the wind's
direction, fell quietly upon my hair and shoulders, one on my nose, one on my lips. I tilted my
face back, shutting my eyes, receiving the snow.

Mansel had died with his mouth agape, the
bearded lips wrenched back from the gums;
and snow had settled, drifted, and frozen inside
his mouth, upon the tongue and the lower grind-
ing-teeth.

I can't soften that rictus, ever, can't slacken
that pain. It is still in me, along with Henged and
the silent castle, and all I have lost. The white
shock to the heart. I unfastened my heavy cape,
and unslung it from my shoulders. Quickly the
mountain-wind reached for my body, chilling me
at neck and groin and armpits. I began to spread
the cape on the snow-covered scree, beside his
body, meaning to wrap him in it. I was shuddering with shock, and crying.

Then I heard Mansel's voice in my head.
Staring down, I imagined the racked lips below
me, shaped again well and whole, and twisting in
scornful sympathy: telling me that the dead have
no need of covering against the wind, when the
living need it. The man is dead, his voice said
dryly in my mind. It's no time for flashy self-sacrifice. You'll be—I saw his lips wrinkle—a hero in

good time, boy Percival. But honouring the dead
should not be confused with sentimentality.

And I whipped the cape up from the ground
again, shaking it free from snow, and hung it
once more around myself, standing up, looking
away from the body. Still shivering, I tried to bite
hardness into my face, and look slit-eyed into the
moderate wind, over the snow-covered boulders,
between dark rock-walls, to where the valley
widened. The cloud level, only a little higher than
the pass where I stood, was constant and firm-
edged into the distance, so that the valley fell
steadily away from it. The pass was a mere tunnel, between the quiet cloud and the icicled
crags. My horse looked at me, uneasy, nearby,
its ears trembling back and then pricking forwards again.

I stooped once more, to the frozen head.

As far as I could, I swept the snow, with my
hands, away from the face and beard. But at
base it was hard rime; scraping at that seemed to
be scraping at the skin itself. Sickness made my
stomach snatch and shiver; once I had to sit
back on my heels and shut my eyes tightly for a
moment, swallowing, my temples and the forehead just above my eyes banging to my blood-
beat. Then I looked again at the rictus; slowly
took off my right gauntlet, and with my fingers
brushed out the powder-snow and broke away
the base of ice from the inside of his mouth. Then
I tried to lift the jaw, to close the mouth; but
that could be done only with some cracking or
tearing at the side of the face. Nor would the lips
pull down.

I didn't brush away the snow from his eyes.

When I lifted the body, it was like the great branch of a tree. Scraps of half-frozen clothing trailed like leaves. I struggled with him, my teacher, to my horse. Then the body was too stiff to lie naturally over the horse's back. Fumbling in the cold, I unfastened and unthreaded the reins, and used them to lash him awkwardly across the saddle. His legs and arms kicked and sprang at the air. Praying that the precarious lashing would hold, I had to turn my back on him and lead the horse down, guiding it by the bridle. It was difficult, picking a way through the snow-covered boulder scree—-much harder on the downward journey. For the horse there was considerable danger; if it broke a leg there I would have to kill it, and so increase the hardship on my family. In the midday gloom I searched for the foot- and hoof-marks. Even uphill I had dismounted for this section and led the horse up it.

The body bobbed, a travesty, behind me. The only sounds were of its creaking, the horse's breath, and the small ring or grate of our steps. When my spur, or a hoof, struck against rock the sound echoed between the black and white crags. The heavy cloud seemed to press us down towards the valley, and public grief.

I went back to the New Year feast with settled snow on my hair and shoulders, making the people turn and laugh. I smiled as the snow melted, and drank more; but for the remaining hours their revelling stayed at a certain distance from me. I wanted the snow to fall steadily all night, to be sharp and firm in the morning light, like the hardness of home, like the morning after Mansel's burning. The white-rimed glittering rock ridge against the sky.

On the first bright day of the year I practised spear-throwing in the open again, and gave instruction to two of the younger men of the house. The snow was not thick, after what I had known in the mountains in other winters, but it had settled and frozen; and now, under windless sunlight such as we hadn't seen for weeks, it lit everything from beneath and beside. Our figures moved sharp and dark, upon earth more dazzling than the sky. We ran, half-skidding, to retrieve our spears, and walked back with our own long shadows ahead of us and the snow sparkling as it melted in our bootmarks. I threw till my thighs and shoulders were stiff with the half-forgotten use, and the target—a bale of hay from the winter-store—was broken repeatedly.

My lady went out riding, with the chaplain and Ranalph in attendance. As she returned, she reined in her horse, dismissing the others ahead of her, and watched one of my throws. Walking back, panting and smiling, I bowed to her; and she lifted her gloved hand in the air, then to her lips, in salute. As I turned away from her again, to address the target, I was beginning a three-month farewell.

The old year, I had arrived at her house; this new year, I would leave—not for ever, but for some time. Here at the start of the year, with the worst of winter still ahead, I was resuming training for my eventual departure.

Did I want her to know that, at this time? After the next throw, when I picked up the spear I stayed a moment at that distance, pretending to scrutinize the spearhead, and looked under my brows at her motionless figure, the wolf's-coat silvery and snow-lit, and her horse's breath making small clouds on the air. I walked back then, and right up to her. Her horse dipped its head twice as I approached; then leaned slightly towards me, nuzzling at my sweaty tunic, as I stood beneath her.

Sun and cold had stirred up the blood in her face, had for one morning loosened and freed her from the winter pallor. Muffled like that and smiling, half dazzled by the low sun and the blazing snow, she looked like a girl still, the bones of her face sharp-standing under smooth and unweathered skin. None of the other women of the house could match that.

'My lord,' she said, 'you've lost none of your talent.'

'On the contrary. I'm badly out of practice. But it's beginning to come back. The other two are learning fast.'

'They've lacked teaching.'

I nodded, looking down. I rubbed the back of my gauntlet against the hard brow of her horse.

'It excites them to work with you,' she said. 'They've gone so long without proper instruction.'

'They'll serve you well,' I said, carefully.

I met her eyes again. Then she nodded, and smiled. 'Yes, I think so.'

She reached down to me her gloved left hand, and I took it, standing against her horse's side, my left hand lifted to the pommel of her saddle, the spear in the crook of my right elbow, my right hand holding her offered wrist. I hooked my fingers in under her fur cuff, to touch the warm arm: *I shall go, you must accept that.* I stared at her glove, my head close to her but not lifted.

'You'd better instruct them in other things,' Whiteflower said quietly. 'Soon: before the spring.'

Then I was forced to look up at her; she was smiling, expecting to meet my eyes: a smile of controlled unhappiness, on a bright day. Generous, where I would so well have understood selfishness.

'I shall be most happy to do that.'

'Good.'

I stooped my head and, rolling back the fur cuff with my fingers, kissed her just above the wrist. Then I stepped back, taking the shaft of the spear in my hand, and stood to see her go. She stirred the reins with her right hand, gave a small kick with her knees and heels as if (my mind saw in a flare) making love; and was carried briskly away.

I shall certainly return, I thought, facing the white fire-field of snow.

5

There was one great snowstorm, in the second
week of Lent, when the days were becoming
longer and it was tempting to think that the winter was retreating. At nightfall a man was missing and there were fears for him. Some, who had
been reluctant to go up on the roof in the
Christmas-tide storms, talked now of going out
into the blizzard to search for him. Plainly they
had little experience of such snow. I allowed no
one out, and spent the evening in Whiteflower's
room, avoiding their unrest since I couldn't aid
it. It was ironic and sad, to find myself appearing
now pitted against their nobility, forbidding them
to risk themselves. But it was like mountain-
weather. To breathe, to keep eyes open, in such
a blizzard was difficult enough. A lantern, supposing it could be kept lit, would light nothing
except the whirling snow.

I lay awake, after we had gone early to bed,
hearing the moaning wind, and snowstorms
seethed across the back of my eyes.

Next morning it was sullen east-wind weather, bitterly cold, the air clear but shadowless,
under massed yellow skies which promised more
snowfall. The drifts were half a man's height,

against walls and stacks: in places draped and fluted in impersonal beauty. Everywhere there was nearly a foot of snow. No-one talked now of a search that should have been made.

I gathered ten men. The missing man's son, who was fifteen, joined us in the main gateway. White-faced and red-eyed, he insisted on going with the searchers.

Behind him, in the hallway, I could see his mother, shaking her head at me. In any case Mansel's teaching was clear against it: for survival in such conditions, neither the young nor the old were suitable. The gathered men watched, saying nothing, as I attempted to say to the boy what Mansel would have said to me in such a circumstance, and what his mother wished. Even while they stood there the grey wind made them wince, dragging the hoods around their faces. The sky in the east seemed, if anything, to be darkening; there was little enough time, perhaps, before the next snow; and in a wretched loss of control I struck the boy suddenly, as he wrenched my arm.

It was effective, of course: it achieved what everyone watching wanted—the men stamping, cringing from the wind, impatient to go; the mother terrified of losing both husband and son. Yet a resentment as hard as the wind itself came like a black flame on the air, at once. The boy was humiliated, broken back to childhood. He screamed and sobbed like a girl. He spun round to his mother; she held him against her and lifted her eyes to mine, not in anger but in a kind of sad relief. I had done what I had had to do, but not with grace. She thought the less of me; so, no doubt, did the men watching. I thought the less of myself.

I stepped, awkwardly, to the pair as they clutched each other, and put my hand uncertainly on the boy's head, speaking his name. His face hidden against his mother, he jerked his head, away from me; and she, half-shutting her eyes, lifted my wrist away, courteously but firmly. She turned indoors, pushing her son with her.

I sent four pairs of men out, in four directions, with instructions to search the likelier sheltering places, and to turn back after one hour, or earlier if snow started. I went on horseback, with Ranalph, the head man. The horses hated the weather, swinging their heads repeatedly away from the wind, and tended to stagger in the thick snow underfoot. Once Ranalph caught my arm, saving me from being pitched off.

After ten minutes we stopped, in the lee of an outcrop.

'We won't get far,' I said, clapping my hands under my arms.

'A little further than them on foot, maybe. But if he's out here at all,' Ranalph glanced up at me, 'he'll not be far.'

The missing man, Brund, had been gathering tinder, but possibly also calling for cider and cakes at one of the nearer settlements. There was a widow he was said to visit, for her various kindnesses.

'Would he be careless with the weather?'

Ranalph hunched his shoulders slightly, pushing out his lower lip. 'He's not an idiot, my lord, as you know. Brund takes things easily, though. He might not have reckoned just what it would come out like. We've not had that kind of weather for a few years back.'

Wind streamed past our frozen wall, not flapping but a dry intensity of sound. I smoothed the hide of my horse's neck, depressed. Because Ranalph was a man it was easier than most to talk to, I said:

'I'm afraid we shall find him dead.'

He narrowed his eyes sharply, lifted a hand to cross himself. It was indecent, his response implied, to voice such fears.

'I pray not, my lord,' he muttered.

But to me it seemed artificial not to speak. 'I found my tutor dead in the snow,' I said. 'A little more than a year ago.' Ranalph shifted slightly in his saddle, to look at me. I fixed my eyes on my horse's ears. 'He had been ambushed,' I said.

'Ah well. Brund's not a man with enemies. Saving his wife, maybe.'

'So, my tutor had no enemies, as far as I could tell. But he was a man who kept the code, and he was killed, by rustlers or thieves—men who didn't even know it.'

Ranalph coughed, and gathered his reins. 'Well, I'm truly sorry, my lord. That can't have been pleasant. But the chances are old Brund's holed up somewhere with his feet by the fire. And we'll freeze to death looking for him if we don't stir ourselves.'

We shook the reins slightly and kicked our hanging horses out into the wind. It hadn't slackened. The sky seemed to sag, jaundice-coloured, with the weight of snow, but we could still see a clear mile on each side, and there were no flakes falling. To the west and a little behind us we could see the figures of two men, one of the groups of searchers.

The snow didn't start to fall again until we were all back within the house walls, together with the body of the missing man. He had been found in the remains of a store-hut, under a mile away. He must have taken shelter there, but in a state already too exhausted to survive the cold night.

His body was free of wounds, and the face blank, with closed mouth and closed eyes. But its frozen bent shape reminded me of the past. So did the previous night's snow, lining the folds of his clothing.

I lay face down on Whiteflower's bed, after throwing off my outer coat, gauntlets, and boots; and tried to beat my mind into some sort of acceptance. My lady sat by the fire, with her small dog in her lap, her hand repeatedly smoothing, ruffling, and re-smoothing its reddish fur.

'It's something to learn, my lord,' she said quietly. 'Things do repeat themselves. Or echo others in our minds.'

'So close in time,' I murmured, my knuckles at my lips.

'A ten years' echo, when it comes sharp and hard, is as bad. Or worse.'

I was silent.

A few minutes later I rolled round on to my back, pressing my fingertips to my eyes; then lowered my hands and stared up at the rafters. The subdued light was a pouring restlessness, as the snow whirled outside.

'I'm afraid I talk about him too much,' I said. 'I'm sorry.'

'What's important to you is important to me. It would be wrong to hide it.'

'You're too good to me.'

I leant my head aside, on the bolster, to look at her. It was the dulled, winter Whiteflower, her eyes always on the heavy glow of the fire; but at the side of her mouth a shadow suggested a near-smile. She spoke again then; tentatively, but with the clarity my blizzarding mind was missing.

'I think that when a savage event happens to us, we probably make it supportable by imagining that it's unique. God, if you like, limits for a while our notion of the possibilities of pain.'

'Which are really limitless?'

'All things are limitless, except as God limits them.'

She rarely spoke of God. I watched her disturbing and settling the dog's fur. The firelight tended to simplify her features, into an idealized mask of beauty.

'Yet the event,' I said, rolling my head back, away from her, 'is unique, really.'

I thought of standing by Mansel's pyre, in the dusk, the wet driving snow.

'This man's death is not to me what Mansel's was.'

'But you mourn this afternoon; and you mourn chiefly for Mansel.'

My hand stroked the sleek skins on which I was lying. 'I begin to think his death will always be with me.'

'Yes. So will his teaching. It's part of you, just as the teaching is.' There was a rising energy in her voice which made me look at her again. She had turned towards me, making the dog sit up in her lap; her hands held it gently caught, her eyes were on me. 'Percival, my lord: you thought you could get free of it. But I think we always find echoes. We've been made what we are by our past, and it's still within us.'

I dropped my eyes from hers. 'We are tempered by our griefs,' I said, remembering words of Mansel's.

'That's code-language. That's seeing yourself as a weapon, being hardened for heroic purposes.'

'That is how I see myself.'

We were silent for a spell. The chamber was half in darkness, lit as much now by the firelight as by the afternoon thick with falling snow. I heard Whiteflower move a little where she sat—perhaps just turning back to the fire's warmth. Eventually she said: 'I don't want to see you hardened.'

'It's a symbolic idea, you know that. It doesn't mean "calloused". Hardened in wisdom, and understanding—and acceptance.'

'But still that particular symbol. The hardened weapon.'

'Well? What could it be?'

'The softened field, say? Something made receptive, and fertile.'

We laughed slightly, without looking towards each other.

'That sounds like a woman's symbol,' I said. 'She's to bring out the grace in a man.'

'I sometimes think women need to be hardened. Or tempered by griefs, if you like. And men to be softened—I think perhaps we're not so different in God's sight.'

She had added the last phrase to draw me. I waited, then said:

'Brund's boy wanted to go on the search. Did you hear about it? His mother was desperate to keep him back. She feared her man was dead, and she was right; and she was afraid she would lose the boy, too.'

'Should she have been harder? Prepared to lose them both?'

'Not in a blind struggle with the elements, no.'

'But in God's Purpose?'

She was half-mocking. I said, 'Perhaps.'

I was saddened at the wrestling of our talk—yet wanted to win it. In my mind I saw the wife's face blurring into her husband's, and Mansel's, and other, unidentifiable features: a blur of repeated suffering.

'Does it seem to you a good thing, my lord, to be less moved by events, as we grow older?'

I lay silent, looking at the rafters.

'If another man's death reminds you of your tutor's,' she went on, quietly, 'doesn't that make you more able to feel for his relatives and friends? . . . It makes you more aware.'

'I'm talking about bearing the grief, not about understanding it.'

'You're talking about becoming calloused, then.'

I spun over on my side, turning my back entirely to her. If she could know how little I was becoming calloused. My perceptions were sore and tender.

She continued to speak. 'I think that you're enlarged by Mansel's death. But you seem to be

asking to be shrivelled. You want there to be no
echoes, no repetitions of that pain. What I think
you need to do is to recognize that you are softened—made more aware, for the future. There's
bound to be equal pain ahead, greater even. And
the pain of other people rather than your own.'

'That isn't much different from what I said:
learning acceptance.'

'But your acceptance sounds like armour. It
sounds like something which would make deaths
and sufferings glance aside, not touching you. I
think that instead of fending them off, we have to
take them into ourselves—the deaths and the
sufferings. We have to learn to live with them all
the time. . . . And not only the past events, but
also the future.'

Her mind moved too quickly for mine. 'The
future?'

'Percival: the death of your mother. Isn't that
already with you?'

Frowning, I lifted myself, to stare at her.

'No,' I said roughly, and dropped back on to
the bolster. 'She'll die when God chooses, and
then will be the time to grieve.'

'When you left her, my lord, you must have
known you might never see her again.'

'That could just as well be by my death as
hers. It wasn't what you're talking about.'

Words clicked in her throat, but she seemed
to hold them back. She became silent.

To think now of my mother dying was simply
to go further in the day's sense of collapse:
falling, caving in, stepping briefly out in the clear
spell between snowstorms and then stumbling
back with a new death and new mourners. Yes,

she might well die before I could return. And—
which is what my lady wanted me to recognize
now—of course she would die anyway. Whiteflower wanted me to anticipate my mourning.

On this slumped afternoon that was possible enough.

At last I sat up, set my feet to the floor, and
left the bed. Whiteflower still sat, half-lit, the dog
still in her lap. As she looked up to me, I smiled
at her and dropped to the matting at her feet,
feeling the heat of the fire press immediately at
my face.

'I talk of myself really, I suppose,' she said,
quietly.

I watched her face. The firelight, making visible the bones rather than the full flesh, made a
mask which could as well be age as youth, but
which would always be beautiful.

'About your husband.'

'Yes, the past—that stays with me. But the
future too.'

I waited, and looked away from her, to the
flames. She said: 'I live all the time now with
your departure.'

Slowly I laid my head against her knees, staring at the flames' flickering light.

In the chapel the dead man's body was laid out,
and his widow and son knelt by it, shivering. The
place was very cold. A candle stood at each end
of the bier, and the six candles on the altar were
lit. Outside it was now dark. I knew the mourners would remain here till midnight, visited occasionally by others from the house, in ones and

twos, who would kneel and pray close to them, without passing speech.

I had entered softly, as I did in the early mornings; and I moved to a place beside Brund's boy, whom I had struck at the start of the day. Once kneeling beside him I kept my eyes straight ahead, looking at the dead man's shrouded feet, and at the candles beyond. I had no need to see the face; the face of pain or death was hung now on each wall of my mind.

I prayed for Brund's soul, and for the widow and boy now beside me. There was no need to introduce into my prayers, that evening, my mother or Whiteflower or our conversation in the darkening afternoon: the context of any prayer would be known and recognized. It is never God's mind which needs to be concentrated, only one's own.

When I had finished, I looked aside and found the boy's eyes, candle-lit on my face. His eyes glinted, neither hostility nor acceptance apparent. I met them for a moment, then got up, setting my hand on his shoulder and tightening a grip on it. He dipped his head away from me, towards his dead father, his shoulder twisting slightly under my fingers.

I stepped behind him to his mother, and stooped down on the other side of her, touching her small, shuddering shoulder, and kissed the side of her head lightly. Her eyes opened and widened on me—she had not known I was in the room—and she reached up both her hands and took my hand from her shoulder and held it; her own hands cold, dry, limp. Gently I straightened up, withdrew from her, nodding. Then I set my palm to the back of her head for an instant, uncertainly; and turned and left the chapel.

The morning after Mansel's burning, older men from the village went up to the pyre at first light, while I was still sleeping in exhaustion; and they did there what was necessary with the remains of the body and the fire, to spare me that small horror. I had conducted the burning, the evening before; they had waited on me, in that; but now in their quiet kindness they spared me more.

When I finally woke I found the day sharp, scoured-clear, with a cold north-westerly wind, a few shower-clouds, and winter sun making a golden whiteness of the fresh snow. Late in the morning I plodded up, alone, in the old men's tracks, to the place of the fire. My face was frozen in the wind, my self cold and calm, by the hard grace of that day. Breathed harshly in, the air brought the exterior glittering world achingly into the lungs, against the heart. I felt then like metal tempered. Loss, and cold, had made my heart gasp like the metal thrust into water, and had firmed it.

In looking up, as I climbed, towards the place of the fire, I was looking also beyond, up the ridge, far up its foreshortened snow flanks to the exposed rock at the top, beyond where I had ever been. Plastered with snow that morning, white-grey when the sun was behind cloud, dazzling bright in the sunlight, it broke into the blue sky, sharper than I had ever felt it before. That was the way of that morning.

After a few minutes I stood where the pyre had been, a level patch of rock and grass where the snow had melted, blackened with ash and some remnant brands. I stood in the centre of the ashes, and looked down at the valley, holding my gauntlet to the side of my face against the wind. But I found there no immediate relation to Mansel at all: could not work up in myself any tight poignancy of association. I was Percival alone, that morning, a boy alone on a bared patch of hillside surrounded by ice and snow, and the world opened away from me, huge, under a great sky of winter-blue and journeying clouds, diminishing into forty miles of distance. To the north I could see the coast, and a fishing settlement I had once visited with Mansel. West and east other valleys, only a few of which I knew. Southward the mountains, the pass at which he had died; white mountains beyond that, grey-golden shapes against the low sunlight.

Places Mansel had taught me; but now, that morning, in the cold, I was cut from him, not identified with him. In my head his voice spoke nothing. I was alone.

I stepped from the half-sheltered place of the pyre out on to the ridge again, and trudged heavily down, leaning sideways against the tearing wind, my eyes cramped narrow against wind and snow-glare, rapidly returning home. Alone, and still sad to be so, I was also sharpened and excited.

6

During Lent it remained generally cold, and patches of snow stayed late, but sunlight warmed the middle of most days. The days seemed to widen for us, as we moved together towards our parting. I spent some hours of every day in training, and in giving instruction to men and boys of the house. They understood why it was, though nothing of my going was spoken directly. Whiteflower understood, of course. Already in January she had talked of living all the time with my departure. Already she held the pain of separation into herself, like unborn life within her. She spoke of it once or twice; and it was alongside us all the time. I knew it was harder for her than for me, because although she could apprehend the ordeal of parting she could not envisage the purpose.

We rode out frequently, when I was not training: the two of us, without attendants. She would show me the bushes and grasses which don't grow in the mountain valleys, telling me their names; and I committed to memory not the names but her lips and throat making the names. She passed me the grasses, turning them in her gloved fingers.

On the branches of the trees there was frost in the mornings, and buds, of which the progress was measurable as we passed on different days.

Sometimes we took with us hounds from the kennels: rapid thoughtless energy, streaking and doubling back ahead of our quiet riding. We rested our eyes on their irrelevance. Their flapping ears and tongues, wheeling bodies; their bright eyes reaching at moments up to us, unaware of our mood. When we didn't take the hounds, the silence around us developed for long periods; or not silence, but sound uninterrupted by our speech: the horses' heavy encounter with the earth, soft or hard; birdsong; the skittering away of surprised animals in the undergrowth. Jingling of harness, and the different creaks of the two saddles. On the cold mornings four breaths made steam on the air.

One afternoon when the sun was warm Whiteflower searched out a place she knew. We had no hounds and we were half an hour from the house. It was a clearing, now returning to nature: a hermit had lived there some years. The roofless remnant of his cell now stood, loose walls of stone among nettles; in the middle there was yet a square of sunlit grass. We made love there, in the open, taking a long time; drawing slowly out of the time the essence of our happiness and our unease. The horses, tied at the edge of the clearing, stood quiet nearby, shifting occasionally, in the broken light under still leafless trees. We lay on our cloaks; fur and hide against the earth. The rough walls made shelter from what breeze there was, and in the steady sunlight we lay naked, in March. My dagger and short sword in the grass beside us. Where the hermit had lived, where God so surely had been, he surely was again. I took her in God's sight. As always; always God sees. But this was a magic place; here a man had lived for God alone.

We hardly spoke, in his empty house. Whiteflower smiled, almost laughed sometimes; rarely was there not some amusement between us, and when a caress gave her sudden pleasure her head would tilt back, the eyelids trembling, and after catching in breath she would chuckle, softly and continuing, at the back of her throat. Her eyes pressing up, into her forehead, away from mine, and then gradually back to me, still in the delight.

I remember what I have lost.

We knew all the time, there, that we should lose it. Unspeaking, we traced with fingertips and lips the intricacies of each other: to learn them by heart. We delayed the joining of our bodies as long as possible, because it would commit us to the eventual unclasping. I drew down from her, to slacken the drawn strings awhile, and my lady turned slightly on to her side, away from me. Above the noise of our separate, speeded breathing, behind the pounding waterfall of blood in my throat and ears, I could still hear several birds singing. Could hear one cross above us with a brief whirr of wings. I lay back, looking up narrow-eyed at the blue sky, fringed with treetops.

The horses, when I lifted my head a little, stood at peace together, but indifferent—both to us and to each other. Whiteflower's bay nosed, idly, in the undergrowth: the long stooped sweep of its neck, starred in two places with sunlight coming between the branches above.

The immensity, and the delicacy, of God's kindness.

I laid my cheek on Whiteflower's leg, a little above the knee, gradually letting the weight of my head sink. She bent the leg a little more, and reached down her hand to my head, the fingers pushing into my hair. I did not look up towards her for a long time, but held my eyes, instead, downward: smoothing with my fingers and then with the whole cupped hand over the crook of the knee, down the white calf to the ankle. It was lovemaking, but under more control: a short retreat: letting the heartbeat return to reason. What reason said, was that every part of my lady was to be loved. Every part deserved more rapt time than these weeks would give: more, indeed, than a whole life, lingering here away from call and code, could ever exhaust. After some minutes I lifted my hand from the sheer outer line of shin and calf, and set the backs of my fingers lightly in the soft recess behind the knee. Whiteflower's hand became motionless in my hair; my own fingers stayed still, without pressure, slightly bent into the arch of her leg, just touching. The air became almost silent: our breathing had calmed, but I think at that moment each of us suspended it wholly.

She might have said, then: God cannot mean more for you than this.

It was my own thought: not departing from a purpose, but acknowledging that, whatever I should go to seek, it was not God's kindness, for that was already found.

She might have said: God could not rebuke you, for remaining to cherish this. I believed that too. But only, perhaps, since he is a forgiving God. Even in the unbreathing silence, I never doubted that I would go.

I gasped, eventually, for air; and turned my eyes up to her, shaking my head and half-laughing, as if in the midst of conversation. My hand moved over to the inside of her thigh and turned her towards me; my body reached back to her. Steadily, still in control, we took each other up again, to the pitch and beat we had lapsed away from; we joined our bodies and moved a little out of the world, where no one could reach us. The blood-waves, energy of being: the finest worship.

After passing through, we became slightly apart, yet at peace. If our future separation could only be so: fulfilled, trusting, having been joined, ready without fear to allow the parting. Sun across the land sealing us together, God's eye upon us.

For that half-hour, with Whiteflower fallen lightly asleep beside me, and my heart cleared and cooled as if after swimming, I believed it could last—that physical apartness wouldn't matter, if we knew each other fully. But the belief originated in the very closeness it hoped to transcend. The mind and the body were at peace together. Within an hour, as we rode slowly back, I had lost not only the faith but almost even the hope. I reined my horse in slightly, once or twice, to fall a little behind her, and watch her.

As we rode, bowing our heads, in at the main gateway of the house, we passed, as usual these days, the old porter, squatting with the chaplain's boy, in the sun. They were making the Easter figures: wooden heads and arms, for the Easter ceremonies. They were newly made each year. After looking the horses over, I went back to the gateway, to see the work going on.

I sat on my cloak, unbuckling boots and spurs, and talking with the porter about the spring warmth. The carving and whittling of these figures were finished, and they were being painted.

After a few minutes, seeing that I was watching him closely, the chaplain's boy lifted his head, jerking back his hair, and offered me his brushes, with an awkward smile. I laughed, waving them back to him.

'I'd spoil your work,' I said.

It was true: the painting was confident and delicate.

The porter grunted, amused; held his own brush away from what he was doing, and lifted his eyes to me, the leathered lids rolling back. 'The boy reckons that what it contents him to do will content others. Eh?' He leant his head aside to the boy, who flushed, ducking his head down over his work.

'We all tend to suppose that,' I said. 'It was a generous offer to make. He must guess I might make a mess of what he's done so carefully.'

'Ah.' The old man nodded, taking the point. 'It's good, eh?' I simply nodded, and watched the boy work. A particular line was sustained, from its first wide brushfall, steadily, diminishing, unwavering, to a trailed thread. And the mask of agony had taken on a further definition. The boy's hand itself looked older, more masterful, than the rest of him.

I said, 'You've been well taught.'

The boy hunched himself still further, exaggerating his concentration to avoid answering.

'Taught himself,' said the porter. 'He watched me awhile, then took over—twice as good. As you can see, my lord. I've shown him how to mix his colours and make his brushes; not much else. Now it's got so I do the rough colouring and the boy does the detail. It's a talent he has, isn't it?'

'Certainly a talent.'

The boy lifted his eyes and dropped them again quickly. Delighted. The most important thing is to know privately that what you do is excellent; but it's also important that others recognize it. Suddenly I thought of an evening nearly two years earlier, spear-throwing in the long enclosure. Summer evening light. Within my body my heart and organs seemed to wince convulsively, taken unawares. Neither of the others noticed.

I stared at the stark painted face, carved horror of grief.

"Whose head is this, then?"

'This is John the Beloved,' said the boy. His voice was guttural, but clear, and not as embarrassed as he looked. 'He's the Chief Mourner, after Our Lady.'

He dipped the back of his brush-hand towards the figure gripped between the old man's knees. 'And that's Peter. He'll be the hardest.'

'Saint Peter?' I glanced at the old man, then to the boy again. 'Why is he difficult, then?'

The boy suddenly resorted to his fingertip, smoothing out a grey hollow at John the Beloved's temple. As he withdrew his finger he held the head slightly away from him, tilting it in the sunlight. Then he lowered it and glanced at me, returning to the question. 'Saint Peter is the Rock, yet he's weak.'

The son of the drunken chaplain.

I took in breath quietly, watching the boy's face; when he looked up again, I nodded.

'He has to look,' said the boy, becoming explanatory, 'like a man you would trust. But also you need to see in his face that he denied Our Saviour, when he was scared. . . . And now he is appalled.'

What a word. The porter nodded slowly. I said: 'The chaplain has taught you well.'

The boy shrugged his shoulders slightly, his eyes on the wooden head in his hand.

'What about the image of our Saviour?' I asked, softly. 'You leave that till last, do you?'

'No!' The boy looked surprised at my not knowing. 'We do it second of all. First we make God the Father, then God the Son. Then they're safely done.'

'Doesn't matter so much,' said the porter, 'if we're missing a disciple or two. I build as many of them as I've time for, without a hurry. But I want to be sure I've a God-the-Father, God-the-Son, and Our-Lady. We do them in that order.'

'So you've finished Our Saviour?'

'Go fetch him, lad. Bring him and show him off to the lord Percival. Go on, boy, it's all right.'

The boy set down his work carefully, touched his palms against his clothing, then swung round, half-running, into the house.

'We don't show them around, see, before Good Friday. But no harm in you seeing, my lord.' He dropped his voice, and set his hand on my wrist. 'It's the best the boy's ever done.'

'I'm the more anxious to see it.'

I leant back against the gate. The sun was comfortable: I was receptive, too much so, open to wounding, after the afternoon at the ruined hermitage. God's kindness had opened me, my lady's courage in silence had touched me; and I had suddenly remembered my tutor, a voice in sunlit evening air, calling conditional approval.

I must maintain politeness. I said: 'How are they different, the Son and the Father? By age, I suppose. But God can't truly age.'

'The Father doesn't show suffering, my lord. If we can, we get something into that face that's somehow above the pain. Almost a smile, it might be.'

'And the Son is in pain.'

'That's right, isn't it? . . . Here he is, then.'

The boy was back with the head, swaddled in straw. He lifted the straw away like a mother from her infant-in-arms, plucking the coverings carefully outwards. Someone passed us, hesitated, and hurried on; I didn't turn. Feathers flapped at my heart, at my windpipe, watching the submerged face tilt to the surface.

A thin, bony representation of suffering. Wood, pigment. Reddish stripes round the mouth and eyes, agony-lines, and big staring eyeballs. I held it at arms'-length: weak in myself, my lips loose.

This, to have come from that half-grown, light-moving creature. The hand was old ahead of its time. He stood in front of me, his tongue at

his lips, the eyes slightly tightened at the corners, watching me.

I said: 'Is it all your painting?'

He nodded, without smiling.

'I couldn't have imagined this, at your age.'

'He has a talent,' said the old man again.

The women of the kitchen were beginning to
gather. The boy took the figure steadily from me,
and wrapped it rapidly again in the straw. He
hesitated; then, as I nodded, ducked quietly
away, past the inquisitive women, holding the
image against his chest.

The old man smiled, shaking his head a little,
and resumed his priming of the head of Saint
Peter, whom the boy on the following day would
make strong and yet weak.

From the morning of Good Friday the figures
stood in the chapel, mourners at Christ's feet.
And during the Easter mass the chaplain and his
son lifted aside, one by one, the disciples and the
Virgin, as if they were great chess-pieces; and the
figure of Christ-on-the-cross they hoisted to the
back wall, where hooks were ready, above the
altar, at a place to the left of the already hung
God. So, he rose from the dead to sit at the right
hand of the Father. I knelt at the front of the
gathered household, but knew the heads behind
me lifted like mine to the high figures. In the
altered light, at that greater distance, the suffering face of God-the-Son seemed less a contortion
of personal agony, more a general sorrow. Not an
object for the people's pity, but an assurance of
enduring pity for the people.

Three days after Easter, I left.

At the farewell feast, the evening before, I several times refilled Whiteflower's cup, so that she might sleep during the night. I drank less myself, and slept less, lying awake for the last two hours before the beginning of dawn.

It was much like the day on which I had left my home. I had trained for that day, had long expected it, had dreamed of it; but when it came I found myself chilled, knowing that those around me wanted me to stay, and that—at that moment—I myself no longer wanted to go. My mother's eyes, heavy-hollowed, still widen in my memory: her hands trembling, brushing purposelessly over me. I had to break away from her with excuses, twice, because my bowels were loosened and forced me to hurry out to the back. A sure start to a hero's journey! When I finally rode away from the houses, up the valley towards the pass, the rain which had seemed imminent for the past hour settled in: a fine but soaking rain which quickly became mist and invisibility ahead. At the top of the pass every surface was streaming, dully glistening in a much-reduced daylight. My legs stayed warm where I kept them in the same position against my horse's sides, though even there I was soon wet to the skin.

I knew they'd be expecting me to turn back, and no one would regard it as discreditable— Mansel himself might have counselled it, as a common-sense adjustment to circumstances. Get a dry start, at least. I carried on, however.

The day I left Whiteflower was cloudless, starting cold. Even at the dawn, moving gently from the bed to bend to the window, I could see that it would be brilliant later, and warm—very different from that day I left my mother. I straightened and turned back into the room. Knowing I had left the bed, Whiteflower moved slightly, reluctant to seem to have woken.

After all those weeks of preparation for leaving, what I most wanted at that moment was simply to go back to her there. We could make love again, and sleep till the sun was high; and I could stay all summer, see her in her summer fullness. I could stay all my life.

I shut my eyes, crossing my arms on my chest and rubbing my sides a little, against the cold. There was blue frost outside, in the half-light. I only had to pray, and eat a little, and go.

I leant over my lady, kissed the side of her head, and said softly, 'In half an hour I'll be back. Go to sleep again, my lady.'

Her eyes opened; she shifted her head slightly on the bolster, her hair sliding underneath, and looked up at me; then closed her eyes and pressed her face downwards into the pillow again.

Quietly I went down to the chapel. Some of the people would be already up, and to them I would say brief goodbyes; but the real farewells had been made the night before, and I didn't want to stir attention again in going. I could have found my way down blindfold.

(I shall return, if I live.)

In the chapel the kitchen-girl was praying, ahead of me. This time, instead of remaining quietly at the back, I stepped up and knelt alongside her, and gave her a slight smile, finding her eyes on my face.

I prayed most for Whiteflower, in her own cold chapel; but also for my quest recommencing, and for my mother. Tight, dry prayers that morning: brief seals to a commitment long made. Beside me, the kitchen-girl was shivering. When I stood up, to leave ahead of her (I was afraid she would weep), she threw out her hand and pinched my wrist a moment. I smiled, hard, to try to put an idea of sadness out of her mind. She kissed the back of my hand; then let it go and hunched herself forward, hiding her face.

In the kitchen they were not weeping, but they were subdued. One or two of the men, I suspected, were glad enough to see me go. I sat down on the bench at the kitchen table, eating bread and drinking goat's-milk, which they had set out for me; and I talked a little, quietly, with the women. When I stood up to go, I made a short embrace with each of them there. The old bawdy woman, the parody-Percival of the evening after the Gagreth victory, pressed loose-lipped kisses below my ears, and shoved into my hands gingerbread of her own making, wrapped in kale-leaves and tied with grass-rope. A gift for a boy leaving for a day's fishing. To her I was only a boy, off on a boy's fantasy. In her arms, I remembered that evening of the parody.

'May Our Lord stay with you all,' I said, awkwardly, at the doorway, and hurried out.

Whiteflower, when I returned to her, was dressed: neatly, but without special ornament. She looked ill but alert; not about to collapse. I kissed her, smiling a little. She set her hands on my shoulders.

'I've prayed for you and will always pray.'

'Remember,' she whispered, 'I've survived all this before.'

'I'll come back. I'm not going to be killed.'

'What they all say.'

'I could be killed here, as well.'

And so might she. I swung away from her; still my mind swings away from that thought—to come back successful, a hardened hero, and find her dead. . . .

'There it is,' Whiteflower said. 'Live in anticipation. Keep the future with you, as well as the past.'

'What I shall keep with me,' I said, 'is the day of my return. . . . It isn't only calamity that we can anticipate.' I took her into my arms.

We hid our faces in each other, and gripped as if to make a joint that would withstand any parting. For a few moments we stood silent, like that. Each of us had a little dignity to resort to, then, when it was needed: it distanced us just sufficiently. We separated cleanly, her hands pushing my wrists gently away from her. I dropped on one knee, accepted her touch, and stood quickly, moving away.

'God be with you, my lord.'

'God be with you.'

God be with her.

7

For a month I travelled steadily, finding good company at nights, and small incident. Then for a period of several days I saw no one. Mist and rain obscured the sun. I travelled in the dryer periods of the day, and sometimes in wet hours as well, to free myself from the cold damp which seemed to grow on to the bones, and from a self-destructive impatience. But in featureless or mildly undulating land, under windless drizzle, I began to believe occasionally that I was journeying back on myself, or in circles.

Where was the sun? Where there were exposed trees they showed me the south by their leaning back from the west. I never went far off my course, and the course in any case was generalized. Arthur lay southwards, they had all said, in the recent settlements. Yet, seeing no other man, and lonely and tired from being never entirely warm or dry, I several times lost confidence. On the third day I began to follow a stream, keeping with it even when it seemed to wind east or west. And that night the air became colder, and dry. I woke before the dawn, shivering, and when I stood in the open, out from the trees, I saw overhead—revealed and smothered and revealed again by passing cloud—starlight.

From the first greying of the sky I was on the move, hurrying with the better weather. I wanted to spend that night in human company. I was foodless, except for the uncultivated foods growing wild around me, cold and tasteless. I had eaten little, in fact, the previous day, and on this day I rode, cantering in the more open places, without food for many hours.

Still I saw no one. There was one hut, a little above the stream where it passed between steep slopes. No one had been in the hut all winter, or yet this spring. The roof had partly given way, probably under snow.

If I had left the stream to search for settlements I should have found them, no doubt; and later in the day I would do so, if the stream itself—by now a river—still brought me to no house. But men usually build by water.

Some time after noon I stopped, where the river was joined by a hillside stream, sparkling over rocks. For a long time already my horse had been blowing and tired, his ears occasionally flattening back; for a long time I had brought no more pressure on him than a slight squeezing of my knees against his ribs. For myself, as long as I stayed in the saddle, picking a course among the bushes and soft ground, I was hardly aware of weariness; but when I slipped from my horse and hung the reins back over the saddle and reached under his head, caressing his blazed muzzle above the active nostrils, I found myself half-leaning on him, and knew myself weakened by lack of food.

I carried a few roots wrapped in leaves, but having gone so far as to unwrap one and stare at it, I shut my eyes and put it down beside me. I sat for a few moments, holding my hands to my head; the beat of my blood was heavy in my throat and temples. There were bound to be such spells, when travelling every day; in this case, it was brought on by my own impatience.

After a time I sat back, looking at the sunlit grass, the river and the trees. It was warm here, in the hollowed-out river valley: the wind that moved the light clouds rapidly overhead didn't reach here. I got up, and crossed to the fast-running stream where it cut among ferns down the hillside; and drank from my cupped hands and splashed myself over face and arms. I drank more, then returned and chewed a few mouthfuls of the pale root.

A traveller alone shouldn't let himself get so exhausted. I was aware, as I lay back on the bank, giving the weight of my head and shoulders to the earth, that I must not sleep—exposed there, on a natural route, my weapons still fast on my horse's back. Mansel, who himself died in a chance ambush, had taught me all this and reminded me of it in his death.

Yet the sleep came, overwhelming, and good.

Now and again I was aware still of where I lay—of the fast water's steady skylark-song, and the slower bigger water's quiet running; of that distinct earth cold under me, and of the hot spring afternoon light warming me—I knew these, delighted in them, and still slept. Perhaps I knew always, too, the small but definite danger in which I lay, so that the sleep's sweetness was sweetness of sin, defiance, that kick of the heels in the face of our own values to which we are all sometimes liable.

Whiteflower, I dreamt, was mourning my death. Not in black but in grey, and not in tears: her drawn face with the lips sucked forwards, seeming simply held in a great and serious preoccupation. But I knew she believed me dead. I saw her out riding, with Ranalph as her escort, to the ruin of the hermit's cell; and making Ranalph wait at a little distance while she walked, slowly, careful-footed, to the open patch where we had lain. She stood there, grey and looking about her, lifting her eyes once to the branches.

To watch this, as the dreamer, didn't agitate me. I was warm in the certainty that I lived, that she would—very soon, it felt in the dream—be broken into laughter and delight at my return; and that she might suffer unnecessarily meanwhile didn't, in the dream, worry me. Supposing I were believed dead, this quiet thoughtfulness was what should be on her— sobriety, sadness, but no calling-back, no recrimination. In the dream I felt no strain of anxiety for her, and no wish to hurry the moment when I revealed myself still living, come back; only tenderness and appreciation. The sun's warmth, the sleep's soothing.

I woke suddenly, in a cooler air, the sun shifted, the afternoon declining; and sprang half-way to my feet, appalled by my danger. I so startled myself that I swallowed my breath and choked, coughing ludicrously there for my life, in the quiet sunlit place, like a man pinned by a spear.

Almost as if I had been really wounded; and the coughing itself was real and loud enough to attract an enemy.

With acid in my throat I crouched, shaking my head a little, searching with my eyes the middle distance.

It was all calm enough: the higher branches dipping and twisting in the breeze; my horse feeding; light on the moving water.

In the dream I had been drugged into an absurd complacency. Waking, I shivered with a sense of danger. Because I had failed in my training? Because I had slept after instructing myself not to sleep? I was irrationally troubled.

It was like having visited death. Involuntarily, in a sweet placidity, I had been taken from my life and purpose; and in the sleep had been conscious only of acquiescence, warmth and settlement. So easily could one lose oneself. Now the afternoon light, my sense of the air and time seemed vulnerable: my life seemed a chance life.

I knelt, with my back to the hillside, my eyes still seeking movement upstream and downstream and across the river; and prayed.

It is a chance life, of course; even now. In men's terms, that I survive is only reasonable luck. In God's terms it might be a destiny; but what destiny is less and less clear. Perhaps only a particular destined death.

It seemed, though, as if I had, always with me, the vivid impassioned interest of God—but not necessarily his protection against the arbitrariness of chance. And one thing seemed always clear: to die and be meaningless needed only

myself. To live and die well, to live God's meaning for me, needed both me and God. It needed
technique, code, and courage; but also destiny.
And the luck of the world.

So, after praying, I swung up the saddle again—
a little dizzy and breathless even in that single
movement—and continued downstream.

And came, within three-quarters of a mile, to
the lord fishing.

The river's shallow gorge widened, as I turned
a corner and the hills sank back, and became a
broader valley with water-meadows; and at once,
still hundreds of yards away, I saw the tethered
horse, fastenings on its back and side glinting,
and the man himself knee-deep in the middle of
the river.

I tucked my hands hastily into the reins,
drawing my horse up quietly, and halted there,
at the emergence from the gorge. I watched him
for a short time, searching the river-banks and
the distant fields for others.

He seemed to be alone. His back to the afternoon sun, with something in his hands that
flashed as he lifted it, and suddenly fell, indis-
tinct. Then he bent quickly, gripping something
from the water; and waded to the bank, clasping
his hands to his body.

He had speared a fish. Standing fixedly, legs
apart in the stream, letting the trout zig-zag
beneath him, and striking suddenly. Now, on the
bank, he beat its head smartly against a stone,
and threw it into a reed-basket. Then he
turned, his back to the light again . . . and lifted

his right hand to shoulder-height, looking my
way, in salute.

Slowly I ride towards him.

The whole valley has widened to meet the
sun, and I ride into the light, restraining my
horse to a walking pace, watching the man ahead
and the empty country beyond him, searching
for danger through my dazzled eyes.

He has returned to the river, wading steadily,
his arms wide to balance him, facing upstream;
and he settles himself again in the place he
favours; his eyes down, concentrating upon the
water. When I stop again, twenty yards from his
horse and the fish-basket, he glances softly,
quickly, towards me—and beckons me silently,
flapping his fingers against his left palm.

At the water's edge I dismounted, and stood with
my hand against my horse's neck, watching
him. He struck at the water, missed, and
returned quickly to his previous motionless-
ness: the spear raised, steadied by both hands,
his eyes intent. Then, without moving his head,
he spoke quietly.

'Food in the leather bag. On the horse. Wine
in the flask. Be so good as to serve yourself.'

I hesitated. Perhaps I was reluctant to admit
how much I needed the food he offered. His
words, however, had in them as much command
as invitation. I turned to his horse: its eye
watched me, an ear wavered, as I approached. A
dark bay, huge and alert and at every point mag-

nificent. Its crupper was decorated with jewels, red and orange stones. I fondled the sleek high head, as I passed in front of it, and the ears were pricked and the eyes rolled forward again, to the lord in the river.

The food in the leather bag was nut-cake, cheese, a small loaf of rich bread, and a moist sweetmeat wrapped in leaves. The wine was rough stuff, nothing akin to the jewels and the costly horse, but cold to lips and throat, warm in the chest, and a foil to the fine white cheese.

I sat down on a flat stone at the waterside and ate, gratefully, trying not to hurry.

The lord caught a second trout, in a sudden flurry of water; waded heavily to the bank, stunned it and threw it with the first. He smiled at me then, shaking his hands free of water. I smiled in return.

He said: 'We don't see many travellers.'

'You give a kind welcome.'

'Good appetite. Travelling gives a hunger.'

He lowered himself, with difficulty, to the ground near to me—one leg extended forwards, the hands dropping to support his weight. I remembered an unevenness in his wading, and saw his right fist pressed against his groin. Evidently an old injury there. He was a man of about thirty, seen like this in the afternoon, still unwrinkled about the eyes and throat; but his manner was that of an older man. His dignity seemed that of wealth and power. Dark-headed, dark-bearded, dark-eyed.

I lifted food towards him, laid out on the leather bag; but he shook his head quickly and lightly. 'That's for you,' he said.

After a moment I said: 'My name is Percival.' He nodded, the right hand clamped now hard against his inner thigh.

'I'm from the north-west—a long way.'

'And you're seeking Arthur.'

Blood rose slowly in my face. I smiled, excited. 'How'd you know that?'

'Clear enough.'

I reached for a handful of nuts. 'Some tell me I'm too young.

'For what?' He smiled, waving his left hand loosely. 'For some pursuits you may be too young. For others possibly just the right age. What do you hope for, if you find Arthur?'

The abbot had counselled reticence. 'For employment according to the code.'

'Slaying Red knights. Solving magicians' riddles.'

'You know the traditions, it seems, my lord. They are founded in a reality.'

I had practised the arguments with Whiteflower, many times.

He nodded, watching the water's surface absently, as if still fishing.

I had met few noblemen. Beware, the shrivelled abbot had told me, of riches and those who possess them. Camels and needles' eyes.

This man was calm in his riches. Steadied, perhaps, by pain: his hand pressed and gripped his thigh, his eyes and his thoughts somewhere else.

'I needed the food,' I said, folding what remained back into the bag. 'Whose food have I eaten?'

'My name is Henged. I'm also called, reasonably enough, the lord who fishes.' He smiled. 'I'm
glad the food was welcome.'

'I hadn't eaten bread for two days.'

He took the bag from me, drawing the string
and knotting it. 'You come from the north. Where
did you spend last night? There are no commu-
nities northward for a good way.'

'I slept alone the last two nights, in bivouac.'

Henged nodded, his eyes searching my face.
Then he said: 'Sleep tonight at my house,
Percival. . . . You'll be safe, as a guest. And very
welcome.' He gripped the bag, looking down at
his knuckles, and frowning slightly. 'My people
are always hoping for travellers. You might say
that you were forever expected.' He glanced up,
half-smiling, half-anxious.

'That's hospitality graciously offered, my lord.
And offered—like this food—when I'm most in
need of it. I shall be very grateful.'

His eyes brightened on mine. He nodded
sharply, smiling, and began to get to his feet. I
moved to help him, but he swung his shoulders
away and jerked upright quickly, stepping
stiffly but at speed to his horse's side. I watched
as he fastened the fish-basket and secured it to
the saddle.

'Is it far to your house, my lord?'

'A mile.'

I looked about us, at the empty valley, and the
yellow hillslopes. Now, in the late afternoon,
almost all clouds had disappeared, the wind had
dropped; and the air was clarifying itself all the
time, so that the evening light would be the

sharpest. At night there would be frost and starlight, tomorrow brilliantly fine weather.

'You often fish alone here?'

'Every day.'

'It seems like an invitation to your enemies—'

'I've no enemies.'

'Or to a chance traveller like me—perhaps a desperate man, prepared to murder. Your horse alone is worth—

'I have no such fears,' he said, steadily, with a gravity which silenced me. With surprising ease he reached up and sprang into the saddle, and was away, leaving me to follow.

His food had strengthened me, but my horse was very tired. I didn't attempt to ride up alongside him. From a few paces behind, I watched him, leading me to his home. He rode slightly lopsided in the saddle, because of his injury. As he rode, he turned his head repeatedly to one side or the other, studying the crop, or a badger's sett: details of the journey which were familiar to him—I realized he was looking for changes. So I might ride in my home valley.

After half a mile or more he looked once over his shoulder to me, and checked his horse slightly, so that I drew alongside. Then we continued together, at a walking pace, our harness and saddle-gear clinking quietly as if in a conversation. I realized that I had grown accustomed to hearing only my own noises, or those of my own horse and trappings.

'And what else,' he said, smiling aside, 'for Arthur?'

'My lord?'

'What more will you do for him, or with him, when you find him? Become the courtly lover, I suppose?'

'I already have a lady,' I replied, softly.

'So young? And leaving her? I see, you've quarrelled.'

I tried to laugh. 'We've not quarrelled.'

'You're afraid, then, that she'll domesticate you.'

Unsmiling, I rode silent. His questions were as unwelcome, as clumsy, as mine of him a few minutes earlier. We could both do to remember the abbot's advice of reticence.

'It must be a strong call you feel,' Henged went on, without seeming to mock. 'They'll make you a quester.' He shivered, a tic of the face, in the golden air. 'You know what they all go seeking?' he said, smiling at me, his eyes restless on my face. 'You know about the Grail?'

I nodded, quickened, but remembering my reticence.

I felt that he didn't fear me, yet was increasingly uneasy in my company. I found him watching my face; when I met his eyes, they flickered and moved slowly away.

Suddenly he reached out his hand, to stay us. 'There's the house.'

He swung his hand forward, showing me the castle where it had just appeared, from among trees.

Stone-built, grey-gold in the low sunlight, it was compact and elegant. Set on only a slight swelling of land, yet it could command the valley and the low country opening eastward. From the distance it was the finest house I had seen,

though a solid thing of nature, stone and earth.
There seemed no magic about it. And it was like
its lord's welcome to me by the river: steady and
still, in warm light.

The lord showed no urgency, in riding on. In
my turn I watched him, as he viewed his own
house. It was as if he was trying to see it as I
might see it; and I tried to see it as he did. There
was not only weariness but also intensity, in his
softened eyes; it was like a father watching a
child of whom he almost despairs, yet whose
existence still stirs his blood with delight.

As we gained the final slow rise to the house,
I looked up to its roof, and to a platform there on
which figures were standing, behind a parapet.
They turned to each other, indicating us; and
Henged, seeing them too, lifted his hand, much
as he had lifted it to me in the distance, that
first salute.

There were large stables, with ten horses there: a
place freshly-cleaned, wetted, carrying a sharp
smell of horses and hay, almost free from the
acidity of old straw. I had tried all winter to get
Whiteflower's stables into this sort of shape. The
stableman received my horse with a brisk gentle-
ness and a shrewd eye. I mentioned, but felt I
hardly need do so, how far I had ridden, and the
horse's need for fodder and a little water. His
dialect meant little to me, when he replied; but
we understood each other by gesture and common-sense. Between us we had the saddle and
gear quickly off the horse. I carried my spear and
sword with me, across the sunlit yard into the
house, following the fisher-lord.

Inside the main doors there was a rack on which I could leave the weapons; and two servants met us there, receiving from me my gauntlets and helmet. The servant who took them, a thin, melancholic man of middle age, knelt momentarily before me and lifted the back of my right hand to his lips. Henged met my eyes, but said nothing. He turned, dismissing the servants, and led me, with his slight limp, into sunlight again, across a second inner yard, and into darkness.

It was the chapel. In a few seconds faint light was evident, from a high window ahead—not far away, for the chapel was small, almost cramping. It might have held thirty people kneeling, huddled together. Momentarily I found myself imagining what would bring such a gathering: a great storm, flooding, a plague. . . .

Three strides would have taken me to the stone table. My eyes were clearing. Nothing else stood on the flagged floor; in front of the table itself was rush matting, and on the table's great stone slab were set seven candlesticks, their tall candles unlit. The room was cold, still wintry.

The fisher-lord crossed himself, then knelt, stiffly, setting one hand flat on the floor as he lowered himself. Then he prayed in silence. A little distance from him, I knelt also; and gave thanks, for a further stage accomplished, for my continuing life, and for this quiet hospitality, which so far I was prepared to trust.

The lord's brief afternoon prayer was quickly finished. I heard him gaining his feet and stepping back. But he would not expect my thanks to be so soon over. I prayed as always. Suspense of a familiar submission, in the unfamiliar house.

Getting up, I felt my fatigue again. Henged held the chapel door open for me. Outside the early evening seemed noon-bright. He gripped my shoulder in the second yard. 'My lord Percival, be fully welcome. Tonight we feast in your honour.'

'Feast?' I stared at him ungraciously, flushed and bewildered. 'My lord? There's no call for that. . . . My lord, forgive me, I'm very weary. What I want and need are simple fare and early rest.'

He smiled. 'Rest now, Percival.' The two servants who had attended us at the main doors stood at readiness across the yard. He lifted his hand slightly towards the man who had waited on me, and called him to us. 'The servant will lead you to your chamber. Please ask him for anything you wish.'

'My lord, a place by the fire is all I—'

Henged's frown cut me short. He made me feel it was a clumsy discourtesy, to reject his hospitable kindness. 'Rest for two hours, Percival. At one hour after sunset we feast.' Suddenly the nervous anxiety tensed his features again, momentarily, bewildering me. 'I shall look for you there,' he said.

I slept a little, sunken deep in the huge guest-bed. Arthur himself couldn't have offered better. The river I had followed all day glittered still in my mind. Then the eye of the fisher-lord's tall bay. And the lord himself, sunlit by the water, lifting his hand in greeting.

Not deep sleep. Several times I discovered myself staring up at the dark canopy of the bed, without knowing I had woken. Then once more he would be lifting his hand to me.

Still he lifts his hand. The greeting is endlessly repeated in my mind, it is part of my mind now. And the fish speared, beaten on stone, basketed.

Through the small window the sunset-blaze made a miracle in colour. Awake, I lifted myself in the bed, and watched it on the matting floor. The pink-red of a cock's crest thickening, second by second, and trembling as sunlight does towards a brilliant crimson, a hot shaft of colour while the room grew colder, towards a night of frost. From there within the house, I pictured how it might look from half a mile off, from the approach which the lord and I had made— orange in the red evening light, the valley-shadows gathering steadily and certainly towards it. In my imagination I was out there, gazing at the fierce-coloured castle, as well as within it.

The matting darkened to mauve, and a purple-grey. I slept again, and when I woke it was dark. Not yet full night, but colourless, the shapes of the room being different intensities of charcoal. I sat up, slowly, threading my fingers through my hair, opening my eyes wider and allowing them to rest in the darkness. I had dreamt, fragmentarily and only just outside consciousness, of my farewell to the aged abbot, at the monastery at which I rested on my journey from home. I dreamt of being again in his small room at dawn, the old man who never slept more

than three hours at a time, giving me his blessing and his dour farewell advice.

'It is not a frenzy, the good life. Contain your
eagerness, within a due patience. The God who
provides your experience is not a recalcitrant
servant, to be shaken by the shoulders. We are
the servants, and we wait his time.'

His loose-skinned, grey right hand, its thin
dry fingertips rubbing his earlobe. 'We may wait
a whole lifetime, while shouting and songs of tri-
umph are carried on the wind from the next
fields. Still we must wait. Keep silence. Trust.'

I wondered if he was counselling me against
questing at all.

'No, no; go and seek. Observe. Search. Always
with patience.'

He leant towards me, his voice dropping. 'The
Arthur you dream of exists, and you'll follow
such leads to him as you find. But you can't
wring him out of your experience; and the life
that intervenes, less ideal for you perhaps, may
be as important for you. Don't badger the world,
son Percival. Don't bore it with questions and
restlessness. Throughout your quest, if it takes
you fifty or sixty years, listen; receive; observe;
see God's pattern for you presenting itself. Wait;
accept; keep silence.'

I make his words afresh in my memory, and
my understanding. I think he didn't say so
much; and certainly he spoke less in my idiom.
His dialect was guttural and strained by age—in
the first day there I had understood little of what
he said. What I say here is what his words
meant—or came to mean—in my mind.

And when he had prayed finally over me, he stayed in silence for some time, standing, his cassock trembling slightly in front of my open eyes. Kneeling, I waited for his signal to get up. Outside—easy symbol of my renewed quest—a cock crew harshly: an arrow being dragged through a wound: the quiet settling in gradually afterwards. Eventually the old man lowered his hands to my shoulders, and touched me with his fingertips to indicate that I should rise. Then I was a foot taller than him, looking down on his skull, and on the remnant of physical life that thinly clothed it. He was white-skinned—rarely moved out of doors. I wondered then whether I wanted such patience as his: to be alive and still waiting, at such an age.

But that was exactly the emotion he coun- selled me against.

As I stood there, above him, he lifted his right hand unsteadily towards my face. I stooped to him, and he placed the palm of his hand against my forehead and the top of my head, murmuring a formal blessing. I said my thanks, and left him, looking once back as I turned to close the door: his eyes were shut; his white, loose-skinned face set calm.

I lay awake in darkness, at rest.

Within myself I was contained, as the abbot had advised: only passively questing, searching my own experience, and settling my mind to patience. So, I must accept Henged's feast, the misjudged generosity of his hospitality; and afterwards ride away, to more houses and more accepted experience.

The shallow sleep had refreshed me, to the extent that I could look forward to the fisher-lord's feast. Faintly from a distance the smell of roasting meat touched my nostrils and palate.

I could remember no taper in the room, or at least no means of lighting it. I lay longer, reluctant to loom to my feet in an unlit and unfamiliar chamber. Eventually the servant knocked at the door, and, when called, entered with a double taper, a dish of water, and a napkin. I flooded my eyes with the cold water, bringing it streaming over my neck. Then, as I sat on a stool, the servant bathed my feet.

'Does the lord have many feasts?' I asked him.

He lifted his head, bony nose and jawbone in the candlelight, and moved it a little from side to side, his eyes closing or lowering.

At the top of the steps leading down to the inner yard, the servant halted, ahead of me, and snuffed the candles with his fingers. He held me back, with a hand on my wrist, and then lifted the hand stiffly to indicate that I should keep silent.

In the yard below there were lanterns, being held by servants, who watched a doorway hidden below us. It was as if they were on a high road, awaiting a pageant.

8

Then it was a pageant. On to the quiet broke suddenly a chant, a thick unison of men's voices; and the singers began to emerge, in file, below me. Slowly, formally, they stepped across the yard and into the opposite wing of the house. They were knights and lords, or squires at least, all of them: bare-headed, some bald, some bushy-haired, some grey, some young. Nine of them in all. The lantern-light plucked, as they passed, at silver: a clasp, a studded baldric, a chain about the neck. Their clothing seemed dark-browns or blacks, uncertain in that light— but fine cloth, which glinted smoothly.

I thought: if the feasting table proves round, I shall believe I have found Arthur.

The chant was a dedication of the evening meal to God-the-Son. *Christ who crieth on the cross/Flesh and wine full furnisheth.* It ended soon after the final man had entered the hall. Then the faces of the servants holding the lanterns were lifted, to find me and my attendant, on the stairs.

He glanced back at me, then continued to lead the way down. Our feet made the wooden slats creak, in the silence which had come back to the

house, after the chanting. I cleared my throat
slightly, in some foolish reaching for nonchalance.

At the doorway of the hall my servant stood
back, his face expressionless, his eyes blank, like
those of a guard—not nodding me into the hall,
nor holding me back. I stepped inside, as it
were, of my own free will; and did so slowly, without confidence.

It was a great hall, its higher darkness remote
and undefined. Only the candlelit tables, and the
ten standing men, were strongly visible. Three
tables were set out as three sides of a square,
open towards me; they were covered—I had
never seen anything of the kind—with cloth-of-
gold, of incalculable cost; and on the cloth were
dishes of nuts and wine. Silver again for the
dishes: shining calmly, moving only as the can-
dle-flames wavered.

I have recreated every detail, in innumerable
recollections. Along the outer sides of the three
tables stood the nine men whose entry I watched;
and opposite me, at the middle, the lord Henged.
His head was lowered, all their heads were lowered, as if for a grace, as if I had entered late. A
place was empty, awaiting me, at the right hand
of my host, a chair of carved oak, like all the others. I stepped past them, took my place, and
bowed my head.

The glittering table before us; the candles
burning and spluttering in the silence.

Henged drew back my chair and indicated
that I should sit, and he and the company did
the same. Again heads were bowed; and a man at
the other side of the lord, at his left hand, spoke
in Latin, a blessing. His voice frail and light, but

clear in the stillness; the depths and heights of the hall did not concern us, and within our light the words were crisp.

At the end of the blessing, no one moved, to eat or speak; but the heads were at last lifted, and I could meet the eyes of the men around me. They were looking towards me, and away again; looking towards Henged, and back towards the far end of the hall. The lord himself, beside me, was still young, but pale, his eyes always fixed upon that distance. Without surprise, he seemed yet commanded by an intensity: I couldn't speak to him. And no one was speaking.

Then he lowered his eyelids a moment, slowly, as if in a yielding or an acquiescence; he parted his lips and drew in breath; he leant back a little, his hands touching the arms of his chair. Now each man was watching him.

And he began to age.

Around me the men began a muttering. A patter of incoherent words, as if they were possessed. It swelled, it became heavily-voiced, all the lips on all the faces rapidly moving, beards and moustaches quivering, shoulders beginning to shake. Their eyes widened and narrowed again, watching him. A blurred, elemental noise—of fear or love, of reverence or execration—surged uncontrolled from their open throats; and a beat broke into it, a jerked rhythm. Na . . . Na . . . Na. . . .

I stared, cold of stomach, around the table; but they were all watching him only. I turned to watch him, too. Na, na, na, the shouting still growing.

Then it was as if the noise created his agony. His right hand left the oaken arm of his seat; he

clasped it to his inner thigh, and leant stiffly forward, bent by pain; then back again, gasping. It
was the first sound that had come from him: I
heard it through the surrounding noise. After
that he held himself almost motionless, thrust
back against his chair-back; the pain wholly
occupying his face. The shouting reared itself to
the rafters, the hall pounded to the voice-beat.

But he was parted from us; parted perhaps
from himself.

Age streamed over his face. Not old, not
young, the house's father; but to the thudding of
their shouts decades of ageing broke into him. I
saw the breaking-down of flesh. Crevices; wires
biting and running, into cheese-face; the
moments blasting him. Decades of age and suffering. I did not reach to him. No one reached to
him. They watched, with obsessed, animal eyes,
as they sent out their lurching voices at his pain.
With their eyes, but with no more than eyes, they
made towards him. Nor were they surprised.

His eyes widened suddenly, as if coming to an
extremity; and their heads swung away to look
where he looked: the shouting quickening, racing, into a frenzy of voices. And from the far door
the procession entered.

The shouting gasped, and at once slackened,
and throbbed away into the dark corners, into
echoes, into settling dust.

It happens thousands of times. Last night;
tonight; tomorrow; in my absence. Its recurrence
isn't measured in time. The girl walks ahead, in
white, holding the silver cup. Her moulded throat
almost dark, against the white low collar; and

her gaze steady, black lashes almost unmoving, watching only him, as she approaches. I am watching her, the glistening sweep back of small cheekbones and temples which ask for hands to frame them, to draw the untouched face towards a lover's lips. She causes me to envy Christ, God-the-Son, her only lover ever.

Behind her a boy-server, holding high the three-branched candelabra, making radiance, on her dark hair. She kneels, before our central table, and lifts the great cup as if for a pledge towards him, and touches it to her lips, though it is empty. The boy, standing beside her, also watches the lord's face, with a strain of familiar pity in his eyes. Behind him stand the servants, in line, carrying the dishes of the first course. She waits, for the lord to recognize her, to nod the progress of the meal.

After the procession, we ate in silence, all except the fisher-lord. It was a dark soup, mushrooms and herbs, fiercely-flavoured. I ate appalled, at once admiring the sharp flavour, and sitting alongside an apparently dying man. He did not look to me. His eyes were shut, the lids trembling. Moist-faced, white-faced, he might have died as we ate there, and none of us stirred for him.

He ate nothing; he was separated from us. His hands did not leave his wound—as if they were stanching a blood-flow there. And it had all happened before: about us there was no surprise. The rustle, the soft clatter; bowls lifted to the lips that had shouted; eyes meeting across the tables and the space between them, as the bowls were lowered; touching, and moving away.

Sitting beside his suffering, I remembered her dark eyes, and pressed, pale lips; her very young calmness, unaged, unsuffering, but darkened. I wished to see her again.

From behind us, leaning in, servants removed the bowls. Henged, beside me, seemed to sit a little easier, but his eyes were still closed, sweat still standing on his face. Looking past him I met the eyes of the man who had spoken the blessing. The eyes seemed to search me.

Listen, said the abbot; receive; observe. In the strangest experience, find God's pattern revealed.

Some sorts of folly may take a long time to find it.

And the murmuring began again. I was appalled and excited. His eyes were half-open now, again looking down the hall. The air swelled with the shouting. Within him, inside his head, was silence, pain-gripped, a soundless state. Age ruining his face, the house's young father; and we all shouting. I was shouting now. All were shouting. Protest or debt, I shouted for his suffering, for the procession and the girl, for the irresistible impulse itself to shout and be released. The rafters suspended it, echo of shouting met shouting renewed. A hung wall of sound, visible to him, flapped at his pain. And now, the second time, the shouting heaved over and fell, as the procession entered.

Muttering on our lips, sibilance, our eyes turned away from him.

Again she carries the cup. Behind her, this
time, a tall adolescent boy, again in white, again
dark-haired, sharp-browed, thin-lipped; his eyes
like hers intent on the lord's agony. He carries a
silver spear.

I and my life are frozen. I don't want to understand. I have the cold security of my restraint.

We ate, silently, trout from the rich river. No
mark of his spear-stab; but he was the fisher-
man. Occasionally now one of the others glanced
towards him. Still Henged ate nothing; we dined
through his suffering.

Limestone-dust, mask-grey, his whole face;
recognizably the lord I saw by the glittering river,
in my weariness, but years older, aged by agonies.
As we ate and eyed him the skull was appearing:
a due of death, a dream of an end of pain.

As the shouting gathered again for the third procession, after the fish-course was cleared and the
wine poured though not tasted, Henged the fisher-lord smiled, terribly, over his pain. It took my
breath, and made my voice lunge out the more,
with them all, half-weeping. He smiled for us, we
shouted for him, for life and courage for him.
From the isolating pain he reached, by that stric-
ture of the lips, towards us and wished all well
for us. He accepted that there was no transfer-
ence of his pain.

For a moment I hunched forward, hiding my
head, my eyes charged; but my throat still
chanted—chanted more frenziedly—the wordless
group-impulse. And I looked up again.

The girl and the youth walked again down the hall towards us, the spear flashing irregularly, the cup glimmering, held against her body. Behind them the raised candles, and servants carrying roasted-meat, under silver covers. On either side of them the watchers, half-lit, the eyes glistening; our lips still murmuring, the sound dying.

Henged, beside me, groaned—then snatched the noise away on a drawing-in of breath. With both hands flat on the table he lurched slowly upright, swaying as he settled his weight, his eyes clenched shut in a grey-white face. I sat a little back, ready to take his fall if he should collapse, but I did not help him. In the silence the surrounding eyes insisted that it had all happened before and would happen again.

His great hand swung across the table, the fingers braced, the veins and hollows between them exaggerated in the candlelight. He reached for the spear.

The boy lifted it to him, well clear of the table. Grasping, Henged raised it higher still, brandished it for a moment towards the gloom above us. Softly-lit, the glinting and precious weapon, against the black rafters. Then he lowered it, letting the shaft slip through his big fingers till he held it two feet from the tip with his right hand only, the left going back to take much of his weight as he leaned across the table. He held the spear-tip over the great cup, where she presented it in both hands, close to her breasts.

The spear-point trembles; becomes awash with blood; and pours quiet blood, into the held cup.

Around me the watchers crossed themselves. I
held between my fingers the crucifix about my
neck. I think there was no sound. The girl's
breathing lifted her breasts slightly (it was real, it
happened in time), hardened the curve of her
small nostrils. Otherwise she was still, the cup
trembling only just perceptibly between her
hands, as it took the weight of blood. She
watched, always, the spearhead, the steadily
welling stream.

Henged's eyes were fixed on her. He was not
released, by the miracle, but the pain had steadied, the tide had turned. His thick breathing,
loud in my ears, was regular. His eyes were wide,
watching her watching the running blood; and
his pain extended into the air, reaching us.

The boy holding the candelabra was watching
Henged; so too the spear-bearer. We were silent,
watching all, our eyes returning always to the
continuing miracle—still the blood pulsed out,
upon the spear-point.

The servants began to present the meat. Near
to me someone lifted his wine-cup to his lips.
Opposite, another did the same.

The blood glinted, high in the cup; but was
sustained unbrimming; the level did not alter, as
the flow continued.

The rustling of the meal resumed, its soft clatter. But I could no longer eat. Their eyes touched
him less often, less gravely. The experience was
receding. Occasionally one of them glanced at
me, Percival, stranger, cold-headed there and
desolate. I muttered soundlessly: receive; accept;
let God's experience present itself in its own
time. The words were automatic and contrary,

and I had begun to understand already (already too late) that they were wrong.

As I jarred back my chair and stood suddenly from the table, it was her eyes which lifted, unhappy, to me; then crossed to the lord's face. Henged, without altering the position of the spear, turned his head aside to me. Recognizing my intention to leave, he worked into his lips a smile, a work of utter courage, related to that grimace of the lips at the third procession. I bowed to him. I tried to speak, my lips loose, shaking my head. He nodded, closing his eyes.

I stumbled down the hall, in the shadows behind the tables. A servant at the door reached it wide for me, his face expressionless.

As I got to the door Henged, away behind me, cried out loud for the first time, the cry of his greatest agony. Passing out, I looked back and saw him bent in his chair, huddled over his wound; the youth fumbling for the spear, where it rolled among the table-dishes; the spilled blood pouring across the cloth-of-gold, between them. Then the door was closed upon me.

9

She danced for me, in the night.

The girl and the adolescent and the boy-server came to my chamber, silently, lit by the candelabra. Towards me they danced, forward and back from my great bed, without sound, light flickering on the circles of their eyes.

His hands touched, like a touch of soft fire, her waist, her shoulders, her temples. Her arms, rising from the falling silks, reached in a pointed arch above his head, haloing his head, her thin smooth arms in the blurred light. He laid his left cheek against her upper right arm, then his right cheek against her upper left arm.

He took her right wrist and drew her to him, and with his right hand turned the white silks away from her shoulders, and folded them away from her body, and drew them quietly away with him, stooping to her feet and into the shadows. Suddenly he was gone, and the boy with him; but light lingered behind her, her body a dark outline dancing for me alone. Towards me and away from me, lit as she turned, hard and slender turning into the light.

Later she stooped to my bed, lay beside me, nestled towards me.

I wept, I was a boy again muttering my shame to Mansel's quiet hearing. I shut my eyes. She blew her hair light across my eyelids and my nostrils, and her breath seemed to laugh, seemed to be a girl's innocent play. She lifted my hand to feel the curve of her face: child's smooth-ness, woman's firmness; I opened my eyes and her own dark eyes pressed love upon me, an attention with which she had watched the bleed-ing spear, the attention I thought she gave only to Christ and his miracles. And my hand, drawn partly by her, partly by its own desire, stroked down her shoulder—thin fragility—to the breast, and then to the other breast, peaks, perfections. Her breath on my face, quickening, seemed real; her lower body moving against me. . . . Even as I tried to pray, to shut my mind, my hands were hurrying, lifting the coverings to bring her in beside me, stroking and parting her legs. Then the night took her from me.

When I woke, I spun over suddenly, in the deep bed.

I groped against the boards for my dagger, alongside me, and for a moment failed to find it. My hand leapt; I was frightened. When my fingers reached it, fastening on the hilt, I wrig-gled quickly up, crouching forward in the bed, on my haunches.

There was no sound.

I listened, my lower lip sucked in. Holding the rest of my body motionless, I turned my head to left, then to right, to catch a creak or stir from either side of the bed. But everything was still. There was no sound at all, from anywhere.

Through the slits in the bed-curtains came daylight.

I waited a little longer; then knelt upright in the bed, and—still sharply—pulled the left-side curtains open. There was no one there. I looked to the door: it was secured by its wooden block. I climbed out of the bed, slid my feet into the plaited sandals which Henged's servant had provided for me, and stepped softly round to the other side of the bed, checking the whole room.

It was full day. Perhaps I was upset simply by having woken late. My instincts found that something was wrong, in the atmosphere. (It was, of course, the stillness, but I failed to recognize it at that moment.)

On that side of the bed there was an alcove, screened by a woven picture. Passing my dagger to my left hand, I picked up my sword from the low table, steadied it in my hand, and stepped slightly nearer to the alcove. Standing just to one side of it, I lifted the dagger to strike, and at arm's length, with the tip of the sword, flicked aside the woven curtain.

As I did so I thought of Mansel. Once I had discovered that there was no one in the alcove, I had time to be depressed by the thought. He was half there with me, checking the room, in the studied technique. Afterwards there would have been, perhaps, a certain overall approval, and one point of rebuke: the dagger-loop, which should have been around my right wrist as I slept.

I laid my sword and dagger on the bed, and wiped my hands, flat, on the hides. I was trembling, as I began to dress.

Still I was uneasy. Then I remembered having slept by the river, the previous afternoon, and having experienced the same nervous shock of waking. I remembered kneeling there in the afternoon sunlight, praying with open eyes, watchful still both upstream and downstream.

Dressed, I knelt now to pray, giving thanks for survival of the night. As always; but this had been an exceptional night. I remembered the central hour, the hallucination, my body and heart almost possessed. To have come so near succumbing was almost to have failed—and in a test so crude. I prayed from that shame. And I prayed, uncertainly, for Henged the fisher-lord, though I believed he might be nearer to God than I could be. His agony was the greatest magic I had encountered. In such a house I must pray most for myself.

After prayer, I stood; and noticed at last that my movements made the only sounds.

I listened for cattle-noises, for a dog scampering or barking, for men crossing the yards, or a wheel creaking. But I heard nothing. I lowered myself again on one knee, at the window. It was narrow, and showed mostly another wing of the house, with a small cobbled yard. The scene was sunlit and still. The angle of a shadow suggested that it was at least three hours after dawn.

Rising, I unblocked the door, and let it swing into the room, while I stood back with my hand on my dagger. I no longer feared treachery, but I respected the technique of survival. Then I stepped out, into an empty passageway. My sandals were quiet but clearly audible on the oak

floor, in the absolute silence of the house. To exor-
cise the sense of stealth, I began to slap my feet
harder as I set them down, and cleared my throat.

Through a doorway, at which I was forced to
stoop and check for an ambush, I came to a
gallery overlooking one inner yard. Half of it was
brightly lit by the sun, the broken line of the
roof-walk marked in sharp shadow across the
cobbled space.

Looking down at the yard, and round at the
other windows; listening to the stillness, and
remembering the plentiful life of the afternoon
before; I began to accept that the magic was con-
tinuing:that the house was deserted.

I found my way down to the hall, the way I had
been conducted by a servant before. An arras
had fallen, at a stair-corner. Lifting it with the
end of my sword, I disturbed dust.

In the hall the evening's meal had been
cleared. The tables and chairs stood, polished,
glinting, squarely ranged. I touched the flat of my
hand to a table-top, and looked—irrationally—for
dust on my palm or fingertips. Naturally, there
was no dust. Yet from the huge hearth the fire
had been cleared, a fire which had been fit to
burn till morning and half through the next day.
I crossed to the hearth, and set my hand against
the stones enclosing it. They were cold.

Standing in front of the hearth, I turned and
looked down the hall, towards the door: as I had
looked from Henged's side during the feast, for
the processions. The hall was calm, utterly still,
the air cold as in the yard. But all solid enough.
Nothing looked magical.

The colder, the more solid and calm now, the more certain it was that the evening's ritual of suffering had been miraculous. But a harsh magic.

I walked slowly down the hall and out again to the sunlight. I was—or this is how it seems in recollection—too tense to be afraid. I was holding myself in, as before, attentive to the experience but not active within it. I stood for a moment in the gathering warmth of the morning light, looking about me with narrowed eyes. Then stepped to the chapel doorway, swung the latch on the heavy door, and stepped inside.

Only gloom at first, baffling my sight. Though ambush in a chapel is almost unthinkable, it disturbed me to be blinded for a moment, to be out of control. I pressed back against the door, waiting for the darkness to soften. The small room was very cold.

No one, of course, was there. The stone table, the seven candlesticks. The candles were burnt low, but no longer lit—as if a long ceremony had been conducted here. Without moving, I searched with my eyes for the spear, the cup, stains of blood; I expected, or wanted to expect that this should be the centre of the mystery, the home of the spear. A place shining of its own light. I searched the narrow, tall room with my eyes, leaning against the door, expecting grandeur. Or a store of pain, of penitence; I imagined the fisher-lord retreating here after the meal, aged almost to death.

Slowly I stepped into the middle of the small room. The roof was high above me, but I felt as if with arms outstretched I could touch the walls

either side. I lifted my sword, in my right hand.
With it I could tap the wall on my right.

Every sound I heard was made by myself.
Stepping, tapping, kneeling.

I rose, and left the chapel, and was blinded
again, my eyes shrinking. Again I flattened
myself against the wall, with my sword ready—
Mansel's death again at the back of my mind.
But the yard was steadily still, the air soundless.

The warmth of the light freed me a little from
the gloom of the chapel. I lifted my face to the
sun, my eyes still half-shut.

I sensed everywhere the latency of suffering,
but not of evil. To clutch the sword, to guard as
far as possible against attack, was still prudent;
but I was, after all, a guest. And the house
seemed, after all, deserted. Magic, rather than
man's malice, was imposed upon me; and its
effect so far was of desertion, loneliness, and the
calm of external things. That the house should
be empty was itself unnatural; that the hearth-
stones should be cold, the arras fallen and dust-
covered. But the stillness which presented itself
overall was natural enough—was neutral. Was
only absence.

The stone in the sunlight was solid enough.
Sun on half a stone courtyard was warm, real,
and shifting with the day; now growing, but pro-
gressing towards the night.

I walked slowly across the yard, aware of the
change on my skin as I passed from light to
shadow. At the far corner, before turning to the
steps, I shouted suddenly:

'Who is at home?'

Still the conventional action, though I expected no response. The noise floated a little, echoing. It echoes now in my brain.

Then I turned, and climbed up the way I had descended, slowly up the turning steps, listening as I moved. I made my way back to the room I had slept in. Water had been set there the night before, with a cloth and a bowl; and alongside them, a covered vessel and a small dish containing several oatcakes. I washed, tasted a little of the drink, which was berry wine, thin but good, and ate an oatcake. I had been provided for—but all of this was in keeping with the hospitality of the fisher-lord. I drank more of the wine, trusting to the code.

Then I dressed more fully for departure, except for gauntlets and helmet, which I had left below on arrival. I left the chamber, swinging the door closed behind me; and, still cautious, I listened again in the passageway before continuing.

As we had arrived, the previous afternoon, there had been figures on the rooftop, watching us ride in. Instead of turning down the stairs, I moved now along the passage, as it twisted round corners, and looked for the way to the roof. It was a continuation of a second staircase, at the far side of the house. I went up quietly, but accompanied by the sound of my boots and spurs; and pushed quickly back the door at the top, stooping through.

The light dazzled a little, but there was no danger: the platform was clearly empty. The blade-edge of the parapet's shadow ran down the middle of the boardwalk; half the bleached oak dry in the sunlight, the dust-grains glittering, half in the green dark-light of the wall. There was nowhere that a man might be concealed.

I took three steps, heavy and hollow on the boards; and looked down, first, into the castle.

Sunlight and shadow. Wood, rushes, stone. And not a bird stirring: no scrape, no creak. It was like a dream, but under coloured sky, with the sun's warmth on my wrists and cheek. It was as if one were deaf, but the boards creaked under my boots.

I turned, and touched the parapet. It was waist-high to me. The stone was well-cut, and little weathered. I stood there, knowing I could be seen there from a distance, making my position known.

My eyes narrowed, looking east by south, into the brightness, then grasped on detail and distance. There was no haze, only a spring rawness of light. Hills on the horizon twenty miles distant were clear, slate-blue; and between was an intricate landscape, palpitating in the heat-shimmer. Low forest, and scrub; the traceable depression, altering course several times, of the small river alongside which the house was built. I could see no other habitation.

I leaned on the wall-top, and looked down, to the assembly-place.

Not a hen; not a dog. In the nearest copse there was perhaps motion, of a breeze; at my own hair the faintest freshness of air-current flicked; and the skin at my cheekbone tautened a little, as if already dried by the light. A brilliant light, and a sane landscape; but the house's life was under magic.

I opened my lips to make a last shout; and then didn't trouble to stir my throat. There was no listener.

I might as well leave, quickly.

Instead, I tapped a spur, without purpose, against the parapet. The small scrape and ringing began to echo; then the vast sky took them. But the stone was real enough. I touched the stone; rolled my hand over, to feel the stone's roughness against the backs of my fingers. It was ordinary, and spring-sun-lit.

In leaving I would not release myself from the magic. I would withdraw physically, keeping its sadness planted in me. It was true that I might as well leave soon as later. But I lingered there, in the warmth, touching the stone, listening to the emptiness of the spellbound air which was free of man, or animal, or birdsong. A slight breeze beginning to touch the skin of my face; and my spur tapping, purposeless, against the solid stone.

When at last I moved, the stairs were gloomy after the wide light. I clattered quickly down them, the spurs rattling; and stepped directly through yard and house to the main door. It was barred from within. I looked behind me several times, as I lifted the great wedges away. Outside, there was no way I could similarly secure it, but it swung heavily shut behind me. Who would next pass through it?

In the stables—by now it was only what I expected—my own horse, and no other, stood waiting.

10

In midsummer I entered an Arthurian area.
Children, play-acting in the dust, assumed his
name—passing between them a real iron helmet, absurdly large for them, making their
Arthur a top-heavy, swivel-headed monster.
Thin, sharp child's laughs came from inside the
inhuman head.

To these children he was, as he had been to
me, a figure from legends, but legends which
seemed to have local immediacy. Their parents
spoke of a campaign four or five years earlier, in
the hills to the west: a month's-long hunting-
down of cattle-stealers who had for years men-
aced the upland villages, murdering as well as
plundering. Arthur had come, they said, with a
dozen knights, and—by wit as well as by
courage—had trapped and executed the rustlers,
one by one.

But where he had arrived from, where he had
travelled on to, they couldn't say. Nevertheless
they seemed agreed that he was Arthur. A big
man, not in his first youth, with reddish or tawny
hair to his shoulders. Over the names of the
knights with him, they hesitated; none of the
names they proposed was familiar to me.

So I went west into the hills. I knew, from what I'd been told, that I couldn't expect to find him there now; but it seemed the beginning of a clear pursuit. But then in the hill-settlements I found that the children didn't talk of Arthur; neither did their parents. Something of the kind of which I had heard had indeed happened, they told me. A visiting lord, accompanied by fighting men, who had given their services to the counter-attack upon the cattle-stealers. But his name was Singsuth. They laughed when I suggested he might have been Arthur himself. In the evening they listened to my own story, interested but puzzled. They were too polite to tell me to go home; but it was clear that they thought my quest worthless.

In the late summer I found, again, a place where everyone knew the legends. Better, one of the men of the settlement had served under Arthur, had known him personally, they said, for some years. I waited impatiently, for the man to return from a bartering visit to a nearby village. Meanwhile I was entertained, as almost always, with generosity and consideration: root-beer sipped outside a wooden house, in hot evening light.

His name was John: a man of about fifty, unmarried, an important figure in the community. As he got off his horse he was greeted by several people, speaking of me and gesturing in my direction. He looked towards me, hesitating a moment, then concerned himself with unloading his horse and carrying his goods to a store-hut.

I clasped his arm, when he finally came over to me, with excitement. This man had been with

Arthur—something Mansel himself had not. We
drank beer together, and he told me he had
served with Arthur for three years, in the great
castle to the south. When I asked for directions
to the place, he answered confusingly—a river
running westward, several ranges of hills—and I
asked him to draw it in the dust. He did so, but
with so little confidence that I decided he had
simply forgotten the details of his journey. He
was relieved to return to telling of their exploits;
yet even here there was no elation in him. His
voice and lips spoke of heroism, of the gripped
heart, his eyes were cold, watching me uneasily.

It was a difficult conversation. Some of the
exploits I had heard of before, and my nerves
tightened to bear them confirmed by an eye-wit-
ness; yet his discomfort puzzled me. What I
wanted to ask most was what I could not decent-
ly ask: why he had left Arthur. And the longer he
spoke, the more likely it seemed that he had left
in some disgrace.

I asked him about Arthur himself.

He nodded quickly. 'Great strength,' he said.
His eyes flickered on my face, and shifted away.
'Great authority. When he looks at you, you
shrivel up.'

These were more or less conventional epi-
thets. What I missed was a sense of inspiration.
He ought at least to feel for Arthur what I felt for
my tutor.

'Now that you are parted,' I said, 'do you pray
for him?'

He stared at me, his brows wrinkling; then
jerked his head from side to side, his mouth
slightly open.

In the night, lying awake, I realized that he had never seen Arthur, never served with him. It was a confidence-trick: the heroic past, developed to impress the community in which, in middle-age after some unknown unsteadiness of career, he had settled. He told, with an apparent personal authenticity, the legends they already half knew.

I was to think of him several times in the coming year, when my own story, of Henged and the bleeding spear, had travelled before me and for that reason was greeted sometimes with scepticism.

I lay awake, depressed by disappointment, and angry at the man's weak presumption. What depressed me most was that he had thought it safe to claim such experience: that he evidently considered that there was no likelihood of a real knight of Arthur's passing through, to discredit him.

His confidence in that was explained, in part, by my own experience as I rode southward, the direction from which he had—the others in the settlement confirmed it—arrived. (I said nothing to discredit him there; I connived at his falsehood, for he seemed in his respected function a decent man, whatever he had been in the past.) As I moved further south, the stories of Arthur occurred less, again, and no one claimed recent knowledge. In one place no one at all admitted to having even heard his name; in several they told me he had never existed, that he was a myth-hero only. They were wrong, I never doubted that: but it meant that Arthur had not journeyed in that area. For a time I thought of turning and retracing my course northwards, taking a line a little further into or a little further out of the hills, my general route having followed the western edge of the plain, keeping the hills always in view westwards. But south I continued; and in the early autumn came in Arthur country again, the legends vivid on most people's lips, including new stories that I had not heard.

I prayed to find him before the true winter. If not, the sensible decision—what Mansel would have done—would have been to settle in a friendly community for the worst of the winter, as I had settled with Whiteflower the previous year; I could be of use to them. But my impatience, churning within me, wanted to travel right through the short days and the bad weather.

Then, in Advent, I received directions again, which suggested that such a decision might not be needed. Suddenly the information was more specific than anything I had heard before: there was indeed a court of Arthur, a castle, and its exact location was described. Not as large a castle as one might expect—but this circumstantial insistence, which several made, only quickened my confidence—it was superbly sited, on a high bluff above a great river valley, the through route southward. I talked to two men who had been there, and who—I met them in separate villages, and they confirmed each other's accounts—had glimpsed, from their kitchen quarters, a glitter of knights and ladies, of exceptional elegance; had seen them pass from the chapel to feasting-table; and had watched, in the clearings behind the castle, tilting-practice.

I heard this, the second time, after nightfall. All night, after that, I hardly slept.

At dawn it was raining: drizzle in the quieter spells, gusts of cold rain when the westerly wind got up; and the sense of a day which would grow worse rather than better. The people tried to persuade me to wait there another day. But there was a spate in my head, a pounding pressure; as I left I was already almost breathless.

There were nine hours of daylight, in which to travel. That first day proved more or less satisfactory: I wasn't cold, in the grey drizzle, as long as I kept moving, and in spite of my impatience I kept my horse to a steady pace, at which he can continue all day. Wet pastures of early winter, bushes and trees almost bare, brown bran-mash of leaves and mud beside the track. To my right, the grey shadows of the land moving up into low cloud, with no sign of the ridge-tops.

Two hours before dark the weather thickened, my horse began to dance aside, arching his neck, at the driving rain, and I took the first shelter that came, a herdsman's hut. The wind got up hard, and dragged at the hut all night and the next morning, with storms of heavy rain. I couldn't leave, next day, till after noon, when the still hard-riding clouds began to separate, to show paler cloud above, and momentary patches of blue sky. The wind was still strong, though the rain had almost stopped, and my horse moved reluctantly, screwing sideways at times. We managed three hours' travelling, then it was dusk again: I found a shallow cave, and there spent a wretched, ague-making night—no part of me or my clothing truly dry, and the night, though mild for early winter, raw and apparently unending.

If the directions I had received were accurate, I would reach the castle the next day, in three or four hours' riding. I thought much of Mansel that night, since he had prepared me for all this. Tiredness and the cold night had numbed my immediate passion. There was a theoretical excitement of my mind, at the prospect of immense change to my life, but my feelings were beaten down, huddled dully upon themselves. It was simply a matter of going through with it. I thought of Mansel's fierce allegiance to a man he had never seen. I remembered Whiteflower's quiet bitterness about the code, about Arthur himself.

But they weren't there with me. Mansel's face, to be honest, was sagging, as the months passed, into a swaddling mist. I confused it now, when I wasn't consciously avoiding such a confusion, with the face of the lord Henged—both younger and older. I had now been parted from Whiteflower for longer than I had known her, and in my memory she couldn't reach to my huddled cold present. Her love, which according to the code I should carry like a banner through every ordeal, was remote. When remembered, it pulled me weakly back. Mansel, Whiteflower, even my mother, were not much with me, as I tried to prepare myself to meet the code-king.

I slept in brief reliefs, fifteen minutes at a time, and for a longer spell as morning drew nearer. When awake, I was almost always shivering. At one point or another during that slow night, I regretted almost everything—every sort of aspiration, the quest, the training itself. Which means, really, that I regretted being alive.

An hour or so before dawn, in fact, I made the decision to give up. And my mind seemed entirely calm and logical, though denying every value I believed in. At first light, I decided, I would turn northward, leave the strange king to more confidently dedicated men, follow the hills back to Whiteflower, and capitulate. To her dry kindness. I found I could imagine it, clearly and calmly.

That was fear, certainly, as well as fatigue, talking in my head. I feared the loss of my purpose, facing the code-king. I had dreamt of him as an artist of my glory, a divinity of the code who would harden and burnish my heroism, test, chase, and approve me, and send me out to the world glittering, infallibly confident: Sir Percival of Wales. Now, three or four hours away, the call seemed cold, troubling. I felt no ardour at all.

So, having waited half-desperate for the first light to come, I was slow to leave, when it came. At that alien time when the eastern sky is becoming drained of darkness, grey lightening it minute by minute while the west is still a sweep of night and stars, I stood, just outside the cave, my eyes half-open, my spirits shrunken, still not knowing what I would do.

Or thinking I did not know. Truly, though, I could still not contemplate my life having no meaning. Of course, I went towards Arthur.

There was no rain, though the land was sodden underfoot and alongside. Overhead, clouds moved steadily, from the west yet, but in a lesser wind than on the previous day. Riding, I became warmer, though still shuddering from time to time. The air itself was mild enough, except when the wind rose.

I took the natural direction, alongside the higher ground, and before long I joined a river which led, after another half-hour, to a larger river and its big valley, cutting through the bare hills. This valley steadily deepened, till wooded cliffs replaced the grass hillsides, and I was asked to make no further choices of route.

I was past choices. I rode dazed, depressed by cold and sleeplessness, no longer feeling myself to be on a quest which I had chosen.

Once, the sun glared through the opaque sky, and a shadow or two appeared in the valley. I lifted my gauntlet to shield my eyes from the low brightness; and felt for one moment that the day might be bracing itself as it should, to precision and grandeur. Then thicker cloud rolled across again, and the valley was dulled again, sodden, withdrawing for winter.

The river swung round a wide corner. Low grass banks; on the other side, steep cliffs rising. I rode on, watching out.

Then, as the river turned back on its general southward course, I saw the castle. A mile away, on high land jutting above the valley, two towers, dark on the skyline.

In my imaginations there had always been shimmering sun, light, on Arthur's castle; and it was always approached through perilous mountains, such as those of my own home-land, and was first seen from the last high pass, far below, dazzling on the plain. Flags flapping; knights exercising in the open light. As I approached, down the mountain track, my arrival would be seen well in advance, and an escort of knights—for defence and for courtesy—would canter out to meet me, and bring me to Arthur. From there, he would give the direction. To reach him, to pay tribute, to express dedication, was all that was needed.

I stopped and dismounted, in an open place where I might be seen from the distance. Leaning against my horse's side, I stared at the castle. No flags could be seen at this distance. No glint of light under this dull sky.

It couldn't be approached direct from the valley: broken cliff held it high, inaccessible. Searching with my eyes I saw eventually a track leading diagonally up to the left, into the forest, and understood that it was an approach road.

The road would lend itself to ambush, I thought automatically. But I was past choices now.

I washed my face and hands in the river, and the cold water heightened the survival-warmth in the rest of me. In the saddle-cloth I had a last supply of nuts, leaf-wrapped; weakly, I fumbled them out, and palmed them to my lips. We were a grisly pair then, my horse and I: sodden cold, and exhausted. At the castle I might well be taken for a minstrel or even a beggar, rather than as an aspirant to knighthood. But they would recognize the quality of the horse, whatever his condition. At least they would feed me, and let me sleep dry.

The track up through the trees was muddy, but had been fully engineered: its built-up stone edge

kept it from erosions of rainstorms. It was the
first distinct sign, in the physical world rather
than in men's words, that a powerful and civi-
lized society was established nearby. The trees,
too, had been cut back in the spring, so that the
track rose in a clear tunnel of branches, lessen-
ing the danger of ambush. When we gained the
level ground, high above the valley, the track
became excellent. The river's grey light could be
glimpsed through the bare trees.

All the time I listened for hoofbeats, voices,
laughter, wood-cutting: I must be near the place
now. But it was a silent winter morning. And I
had seen no one now for a full day and night.

The castle appeared, bulked through the
trees; and, a little foolishly, I kicked my horse
forwards suddenly, so that we trotted into the
open—active, alive. Into open desolation.

It had happened some time this year. Very quickly, while still cold-headed with shock, I thought
of the cut-back trees: work likely to have been
done between Easter and Trinity. Next year they
would grow wild.

Only the stone still stood. Thick walls: but
they had been breached somehow, and were
down on the side nearest to me. The towers
were intact. Fixed in the stonework were the
stubs of beams, charred black. It had been a
huge place, twice the size of Henged's house.
Arthur could not be defeated. . . . Yet I couldn't
refuse to see the grandeur of the castle, and
couldn't ignore its reputation.

I dismounted, settled the reins on my horse's
back, and set out on foot, to cross the ditch and

make my visit to the so-said Arthur's castle. I crossed on a sodden beam, which seemed to have fallen from the main gate, and entered, over the ruins of the arch.

Next year, weeds would grow high, softening, taking the place back towards being no-place, a place like any other. At present it was all disaster, an emblem of trapped suffering. Charred wood fallen across blackened and whitened bones, of men dead before the fire. Across their skulls, stretched half-masks of black skin. I crossed myself repeatedly, gripped the crucifix round my neck. By one I knelt, and put out a hand to touch, but couldn't. Bits of prayer were fluttering on my lips. In the one chamber I counted seven recognizable skeletons.

Slowly, I clambered into other parts of the castle. I was weak enough to lean my grip on the remnant walls. My steps grated and crashed, loosening rubble, and ash-mould frothed at my ankles. But there were no certain indications, no rings, gold, silver-work, weapons. Whatever might have survived the fire had been taken, by the conquerors themselves, or by later pillagers. That was normal, dryly normal: it meant there had been no magic in the defeat; there had needed no magic to end this civilization.

I stepped through a broken outer wall, to the cliff-edge. Wind pressed me back. A castle so commanding the valley was necessarily exposed. Northwards the deep valley, channelled by its river, along which I had come, thrust back into the hills—its sides forested, the tops of the hills barer, with grass and thorn-scrub. Southwards the river and cliffs continued, but widened; and

beyond, under that dull sky, there lay a silver
brightness: light falling upon water. A flash from
my homeland—it was how the northern sea used
to show, when seen from the mountain ridge
above my mother's home. To glimpse this other
estuary, after twenty months of journey, from
this defeated command-post, was unmannmg. I
crouched against the jutting rock, my eyes narrowed, looking at that light, with my eyes water-
ing in the cold air.

Yet again, Mansel's death lurched upon me, in
the affinity of half-despair. The frozen, cloud-
pressed pass; and the rigid hulk of the man who
had taught me to aspire. Turning away from the
wind and the silver light, I stared up at the cas-
tle-hulk, rolling and falling always towards the
clouds, and, already chill and bitter, I thought
that it seemed as if one gained, under God's ironic purpose, only to lose. One learned—learned
nobility and code and the ideal of quest—only to
discover defeat, the victory of death and
ignorance. Mansel's death—perhaps a matter of
mere chance (though that too must be laid at
God's door)—at the hands of codeless and desperate men. This castle gutted for no reason that
I could know. For the world's envy for what it
could not emulate.
    I had learned only my lack of learning, my
failure to know men, my knowledge of nothing.
    It occurred to me (there's no hiding here, and
you may have guessed already) then to plunge
from the cliff, as a response to the surrounding,
wind-beaten silence. I thought I had reached the
lowest. I looked again, narrowing my eyes, at the

vast valley and the far sea; and remembered the
spring morning at Henged's house, myself alone
among the magic, the world glittering and waiting. This now was the antithesis, but I felt no
magic here. Only the abandonment of the code
which was our hope; the death of Arthur; the
invasion of meaninglessness.

Well, I would continue to live. At the estuary,
and probably on the way there, I would find settlements. Since I was to live, since I was to continue as if I still had God's attention, I needed to
eat and rest.

I stepped back into the poor shelter of the
broken walls, and began to pick my way towards
the main gate. I believed I had visited each part
of the ruins; then, ahead of me and to the right
of the gate, at the eastern end of the castle, I saw
an arch still standing, though the stonework
about it had fallen, and an enclosure beyond. It
was the castle's chapel; and if this had been
Arthur's chapel, this had been where Arthur met
with God.

I hesitated before making my way in; and having entered I stepped just aside and stood, the
iron-framed shell of a great door near to me, and
looked towards the eastern end. For the first
time among the ruins I was entirely out of the
wind: there was a blank calm in the wrecked
chapel. I dipped my knee and made the sign of
the cross, towards God's end, though it didn't
seem a likely meeting-place now.

No one had died here. I was glad of that. But
there had been wood, which had freely burned
and left drifts of ash and imprecise outline-
shapes ready to crumble. At the eastern end the

roof had half-fallen and the wall seemed to hang inwards; there were blackened angles and shapes buckled together arbitrarily, or so it seemed. Then, as I moved towards them, I recognized among the wreckage and under an immense beam the charred shape of a cross. The totem of Arthur. Or of whatever king had worshipped here.

There had been an altar-table, and the cross had hung, probably, on the wall above it. Breathing heavily, I reached in among the slewed shapes. I stepped in amongst them—light-headed, into an obvious unsafeness—and found my footing burst and collapse under me, my body too weak and feathery to correct my balance. The wreckage muttered and heaved; the beam thudded on to my kneecap, wrenching me down; and in the pain that followed I whined for death.

11

When the falls are in spate the sound is deafening. In gloom, among the steep rocks and trees, the massive flare of white water darkens the real day: it seems to be all the light and all the sound that are real. It floods and scours the sockets of the eyes, it bangs in the brain cavern, and in the rib-cage and the guts and the muscles of the witness it seethes and churns. And goes on. Such energy and such violence would in a man be soon spent, but high above the glinting river is full under the dull sky, sleek and rapid towards this calamity, or this glory— there is always more water; and as long as you stay it will always bang in the brain and possess the air and weaken the daylight. And make your power absurd.

Well, it's easy to walk away. Gradually the thunder recedes behind you.

But sometimes it isn't easy. The aching skull is bewitched by that immensity, by its din, and because it is unceasing. And the terror attracts: the rock-whorls smoothed by immeasurable pressure bellow for you, for your slight energy to join that greatest energy and explode downward

without self, without the feebleness of personali-
ty. Such places are named for the Devil.

This pain was of that quality. I can only speak
of it through that image: spate, incessance, and
the wish to be out of one's mind.

Meanwhile the air was calm, in Arthur's
chapel. I heard the wind, but little of it reached
me where I lay, trapped by the beam. The
absence of event in the world could only intensi-
fy and mock my suffering. When I opened my
eyes from a spasm, the vision was always the
same: smoked walls, stumps of rafters, and the
steadily thrusting clouds. The clouds were not
actually the same, but essentially the same.

Similar might be all event, even if I could
know and see it. To me on that ironic deathbed,
essentially the same.

The injury wasn't mortal. The pain itself indicated the life in the limb; I sensed it all, to the
toes. With Mansel there to lift the beam, and
splint the leg, and have me transported home to
Whiteflower (my mind and my history were blurring, folding together) I might within two months
have been on the quest again. If I had still
believed in the quest, or in the meaning of action.
In that place of all places, with that force banging across the cavern of the brain, I couldn't
believe. Instead, I was likely to die there, and
fairly soon. I knew about men's brief survival in
the open when wet and unfed and exhausted,
though I didn't know how much briefer it might
be when they had also lost belief and purpose. It
would be soon. The nights, at that time of the
year, are twice as long as the days; if the spate
beat on all night I wouldn't want to live.

For various periods that day I did escape from the pain, in coma. And dream-images began to shout soundlessly through the crashing water. Brund, the man who died in the blizzard from Whiteflower's house. Mansel massaging my leg, when I was a boy, and nodding at my cries; and holding my mother by the shoulders, persuading her, one day when she was reluctant to let me ride to the coast with him. And Whiteflower's weary voice, speculating on the way her husband might have died. These images were little relief. The spells of total unconsciousness were kinder, and each one helped me towards death.

In the late afternoon, with dusk growing into the air, my mind was reasonably clear and the pain seemed also diminished. I was shivering, and noticed it and had wit enough to fasten my skin-jacket more closely round me. The training to survive was deep in me, and I couldn't deliberately die. If I had gone from the cliff-top, I should have saved myself great pain; but it had never really been a possibility.

I found myself thinking, not in a dream but lucidly, of the abbot. Listen; receive; observe. God's pattern for you will present itself. And—with the bluff of a lifetime's experience—the Arthur you dream of exists.

Well, maybe he had existed. But God's pattern! All the goodness I had known, I had left behind me; which seemed less like God's pattern than my failure to relish his provision for me. Always I had favoured action, change, quest; and it had brought me to the great castle to find it devastated; and to the chapel, to a ludicrous prostration at a burnt altar; and towards my own death, in a state not of belief, nor even of solid disbelief, but of nothing.

As it faded, I wondered whether I would see daylight again.

God wasn't with me. As the pain beat out of the darkness again to overwhelm any other impression, I couldn't feel sure that God had ever been with me—not even a malicious God. Nothing as intimate and human as malice seemed carried on the largeness of the night or the insistence of that pain. They spoke either of an immense and grand cruelty, or of a vast indifference. Percival was simply not of interest to God.

I prepared my dagger, for the possibility of a stray wolf. If they came in a pack it would be useless.

Strangeness was with me through the night. I wasn't aware of having slept, nor of being clearly awake. I was ill at a stage where the mind doesn't possess itself, but is, intermittently, possessed.

Some of the figures which came were utterly strange: creatures from legends or fables which I'd never heard—or which perhaps I'd simply forgotten. And my horse carried on with me a pedantic debate, shouted across the ruins: he had grown officiously impatient. . . . And I became certain, in that deluded certainty which wine or some herbs create, of destinies:

my mother, exposed on an open mountain;

Whiteflower wrestling in bed with her husband, a hairy man like a serf, not a knight;

the kitchen-girl at Whiteflower's house, whom I met sometimes in the chapel at dawn, revealed as the girl of the magic procession, at Henged's house; and I had violated her in the night, a horror to myself as well as to all others, and was driven out by Henged and a host of followers, who constantly overtook me, my riding impossibly slow because of the agony of my trapped leg. . . .

Such dreams, even when known as dreams, excoriate. They soil the waking self; and though they're healed by morning prayer and a decent self-knowledge it's often some days before their scabs harden and brush off unnoticed. The pain in my leg was no longer paramount; only a grotesque and confounding nuisance. The mockery of the mind was the misery.

I didn't know if the dawn, as it brokenly gave dimension to awareness, was part of the hallucination; nor if I'd prefer it to be. But in fact when the day was light, and a steady rain falling, I was still alive. I no longer shivered or felt cold, but slow and idle, in an absurd world. There had been no wolves, and death would come softly now, before the next nightfall. I had wit enough in part of my head to recognize that this relative comfort, the recession of the pain, the absence of cold, was part of the descent towards dying: one of the merciful mechanisms.

In one of the night's fantasies I had made some convulsive movement—not of the leg, of course, but of the upper part of my body—and had shifted a few inches and slumped sideways. I found myself looking at a black Christ, half-hidden among the charcoal and dust. The burnt still-suffering head of the big crucifix: blackened, the grain split open in silver threads, but still clear in the form of the head, the downcast eyes, the thorns themselves. I was living, and he was dead: a wooden totem essentially destroyed by fire; but such was the sculptor's skill, or the fire's irony, or such was my mind's delusion, that his suffering then seemed more real than mine. And even more familiar.

The dreams recurred, as I was less and less able to resist them. The rain stopped, and there was sunlight for a time, which played on the angles of the wet burnt wood, and glistened on my buckle. It had no interest in me, or in the head of Arthur's Christ. We happened to be there.

After the sunlight came a girl. She was young and half-dancing, with long yellow hair which she held in one hand like a plaything, and I understood her as part of the strangeness, one of the gentler hallucinations. I shut my eyes.

Her arrival, however, had a precision of sound, a reality, which made me look for her again. She was not there. But there was movement behind me; and she came into view again— entirely real, dumpier and scruffier than a dream, with a smear of charcoal on her shoulder.

A peasant girl, tall enough to be my own age, swinging a switch of birch from side to side apparently aimlessly, apparently for the whip-sound on the air. I tried to call to her.

Whatever noise I contrived to make, she heard it. But she turned without surprise and stared at me almost placidly, still flicking the switch at the air. She had already known I was there.

She had seen the horse, and come here for that reason. Once or twice in the night I had thought I had heard a creaking or blowing which suggested the horse was still there, neither vociferous in words as in my dream, nor run wild as many would have done.

I was muttering to her, and with my hands calling her over to me.

Her slowness to respond seemed again dream-like, but I was sure she was real, and, after all, I was beginning to hope. The pain itself seemed to sharpen again, as if I was moving back to life. Either she would free me herself or, if unable, would hurry back to her settlement and return with men who could quickly do so. There would be shelter, warmth, food, nursing. I would be Percival again, would still have a destiny. I jabbered, faint-lipped, at the slow girl, and the notion of God's indifference was flung away on a wind of relief. The pain of my trapped leg blazed at me, a great grievance, a wrong to be righted; and my mind seemed to have cleared and hardened into a flaring hope.

But the girl was laughing.

She came towards me, swaying dangerously in and out of the fallen timbers. I gasped warnings to her. A devil spat into my head the risk of her slipping and becoming trapped, exactly like me: the two of us sprawled, like zanies in a play, alongside the charred crucifix.

She didn't fall, but I began to see that we were in an absurdity anyway. She stood behind the beam that pinned my leg, leaning on it, and laughing.

It wasn't a matter of dialect: my words weren't important, she could see my predicament for what it was. God had granted me the luck to be found; but out of some infinite cruelty, that even in dying I couldn't expect to comprehend, had allowed only madness to find me.

She spread her hair, with her fingers, wide across the beam, fanning it out, and glancing at me. She was displaying her pale hair, like flowers, for me.

I rolled up my eyes, to the sane sky. Today, a light heaven: white clouds, opening and closing upon blue, and a sense of sunlight above them. And I tried to fix my thoughts on my lady, Whiteflower; not on the mad girl or the cupbearer. Whiteflower and I in the quiet ruins of the hermitage. God with us, entirely kind.

The girl was whispering to herself, or to her own hair.

I didn't resent her; only the cruelty which had led her. She was fully grown, but a child in mind, to be pitied.

I had to try once more. Gently, as to a child. My voice had no strength anyway, but I tried to shape my words clearly and without strain.

'Darling,' I said. 'Listen to me, darling.'

There was a faint check in her soft mumbling, a slanting aside of her head; but she continued to thread her long hair with her fingers, making shapes and unmaking them. Then she looked at me, blinking; and seemed to see my state afresh; and burst again into laughter.

'Go home,' I said, as steadily as I could. 'Tell them there's a man here. Tell them I need help. . . . Go on, darling. Go home and tell them.'

She pressed her hair together with her hands and threw it back over her shoulder, giggling; then stepped round the beam, to me, looking down at me. For merest scraps of time, there seemed to be some seriousness in her eyes, but the laughter was hardening her throat again, she was still wild.

'I shall die,' I said very softly, 'if you don't tell them.' But she didn't receive the words. She swung a leg across me and stood, straddling my chest, reached down, and suddenly bundled her shift up high in her hands, above her waist, and crooked her knees wide apart, baring herself above my eyes, with a great shriek of laughter like a nearby cockerel. She was sore and inflamed and had perhaps bled recently. I shut my eyes and pressed my hands to my face.

That was the last insult. She stayed a little longer, but nothing would make me open my eyes or acknowledge her further; and if this, I thought, was what was sent to mock my dying I would never open my eyes again. I heard her move away, through the ruins, and heard my horse—helplessly loyal—whinny in the distance, as she passed him. Then the silence, though it held no hope, was blessed: I would settle for silence.

I don't think I was conscious much more. I think I did open my eyes again, after a period of sleep, forgetting any intention not to do so; and the sick, ruined place was calm enough. I also think I made, dryly and with little hope, some sort of prayers; for the people I had loved, if they were still living, and for Mansel. I would have wished to pray for Arthur, but I had after all no knowledge of him. I hope I prayed for the mad girl. I don't remember praying for myself; the fate of my own soul seemed, at that most important time, an issue of no interest, not even a real issue at all. The great indifference washed steadily into my brain.

12

Here I pause in the narrative. Stillness and silence in the room, then the slight stirring of people shifting themselves: a cough; perhaps the passing of wine or beer or cider, depending on the house and the region. Usually it is night by now, and either the place is unlit or there is a single candle, its rough animal smell the firmest thing in the air, which is otherwise full of my strangeness.

I am bound to be strange to them. But they are gentle or at least well-meaning, and respectful of me—sometimes too much so (it is hard explaining that you aren't a holy man, when it is known that you have what may be called a holy purpose). I'm strange to myself, in many ways. I didn't choose this life, though I am now glad of it.

Children, staring with deep hollow eyes towards the light, tend to think it is the end of the story, and that I'm a ghost. They glance quickly at their elders, to see if it is appropriate to be afraid, and discover that it isn't.

Their elders know that I am physically real, and simple enough; they know that I am still young and in many ways inexperienced, and yet that I have been in contact, more fully than

many of them, with death and absurdity. They
nod slowly, or murmur together. When the narrative ends—drifts, as this in a moment will, into
the present and the unachieved—and the questions, not many of them usually, are over, some
of the older people grip my hand or my shoulder,
as they leave, or pull my head down towards
theirs and press their lips to my forehead. Often
they are smiling, and often frowning, and often
both at once.

Most of them know the story already—both
what has happened and what I dream and
intend—and are not impatient. A man leaves to
look to a cow expected to drop her calf, and
returns, with rain on his shoulders and a piece
of the night wind coming in at the door with him,
making the light flutter. A woman lifts her child,
who fell asleep before I reached Henged's house,
and carries him carefully, stepping between the
visitors, to a crib in the corner. I drink steadily,
and watch their eyes and faces, but don't speak,
saving my voice, which is dry from the narrative.
Sometimes I wonder with some heaviness how
many more such evenings there will be. Fifty? A
hundred? Much longer than that, and the story
will become stale well ahead of me. I worry about
a day when people no longer believe in my search
or its aim, though they may still have the dry
grace to believe in my belief in it.

But meanwhile, I have sympathy, and concentration. The room settles, they offer me their
stillness again.

You all know where I am travelling now. Black-
armoured, overdue, picking up hints of direction

and following them till they peter out. Some of
you have seen me three times, in the same village, returning on my tracks after a false trail.
You are patient with me; if you're amused you try
not to show it. It is clear that a good many of you
pity me.

Reserve that pity; there'll be a time. Pity the
fisher-lord, whom I cannot find—though that I
shall find him at last is a certainty.

When I show you my spearhead, and talk of a silver spear pouring blood, you think me a little
crazy. Your eyes on mine, and flickering back to
the ordinary metal, and to me again, in the
firelight. Magic and craziness are hardly distin-
guishable.

The crazy girl taught me my destiny. More
and more, it seems a parallel; after my dryness
and doubt, I believe all might yet be a pattern of
God's. When I lay with the trapped leg in the
ruined chapel, dying in an absurdity, the girl
came like a God-sent hope: young, active, able
either to release me herself or fetch the release
quickly. But, crazy, she did not understand, or
seemed not to; and I retreated into silence and
shut eyes; and she left, apparently retaining
nothing. I doubted if she could even speak; and I
gave up hope. Not quite the same as despairing:
I let myself settle, without any more pain, into
what now emerged as God's grey neutrality.

In fact, however, the girl could speak, in ways
her family could understand; and, very late, she
did remember and did interpret what she'd seen.
At dusk they turned out, with a cart, and hurried
the half-mile to the castle. They found my horse,

still waiting—after a day and a half—where I had stationed him, my spear still on his back. The girl and her father and her brother found their way across to the ruin, and reached me. And took me for dead, at first. I had lost all consciousness, and take this all from their account. For the three of them it was an easy matter to lift the beam, but when that was done they couldn't find my pulse, and the chill of my body suggested death. It was the father who decided, when he put his cheek to my lips, that he sensed warmth and life there.

Several times, when I was recovering at their house in the following days, they told me, laughing and proud, of the awkwardness of getting me across the ditch, where a fall would have been the end of me: it was dark, the log was slippery, finally the boy waded up to his waist, supporting my body. Then there was the cart journey, the boy and the girl walking either side, in the night, cradling my head and the injured leg to protect them from the jolting.

They brought me back to life: like nursing back fire when only the last embers remain. The mother and the father took me into their bed and slept either side of me that night. My body was cold for hours, but at last in the early morning it seemed to them to gain warmth, and soon afterwards—though I can remember nothing of this either—I was able to sit up, mutter a little, and swallow. They gave me a warmed honey-drink, precious to them; and the drink I do remember, from the afternoon of that day, when I was conscious, dreamy-weak, glad to nibble

slowly their heavy bread and to drink of that tin-
gling sweetness.

With the leg I was lucky: a cracked kneecap
can be utterly disabling. The man had seen fighting on several occasions—he had been employed
at the castle from time to time—and had learned
to dress wounds, to strap up injured limbs, and
to set a splint. Directly thanks to him, I can now
walk at least nimbly, and ride as well as ever. The
stiffness is taken by most people for evidence of
some heroism. Eventually I always tell them that
it dates from a day of desolation, a day that
stripped me of every confidence.

The pattern, if pattern it is, concerns the girl.
My hope, when she drifted into the castle's ruins;
my blankness, when she left without appearing
to understand; and my rescue after all. For her,
in her damaged mind, no meaning exists in the
world; and she has no sense of her own identity.
Yet just in time her mind pieced together my
need, and she brought the others quickly, to
find me.

Once I thought I would find the fisher-lord
quickly.

The first evening, when I was still cloudy-headed,
thanks and invocations were offered for me, at
the family's customary prayers. It was a one-
room house: prayers were made round the same
table from which they ate. During the first days
of my stay they shifted the table towards the bed,
so that as I lay I could be part of the circle.

The father prayed, that first evening, knowing
that I was too weak. He prayed in slow slack
phrases, which seemed to come from the side of

his bearded mouth. A small wooden cross was pressed and clenched in his swollen hands. Gloom about us, the hands silhouetted against the house fire, no other lighting; the faces just visible at moments, or as the head moved a little. All had their eyes shut; but I watched them. The boy's eyes, a couple of times, opened, and searched my face; but the girl was locked in the ritual of prayer, head stooped over bunched hands, the calmest person in the room. I watched them, my mind almost without the energy of thought.

I was cut off from prayer, myself. I was still in the blankness, the indifference, the apathy. I murmured the formal closing together with them, shutting my eyes then; but murmured it for them, not for God.

Attribute that to the weakness of the first day; and you would expect—perhaps I too expected—that as my strength recovered so I should begin to meet God again. Well, it didn't prove so; and that old radiance of my adolescence is as elusive now for me as Henged's house itself. I pray, indeed, and do so sincerely, soberly, but I pray towards the radiance of the past, which I've left behind; and towards the future, the long wound that needs me, the radiance which my coming home may bring—myself dull-armoured, unlit, subdued.

Even in the search for Arthur I had never forgotten that empty house on the sunlit May morning, and its unfinished magic. As an Arthurian knight I hoped to return, glittering, in God's grace, and would complete what I had left incomplete. I couldn't be clear what would happen, but it would be a question of releasing a man from suffering, and it would be heroic.

I stayed eight weeks, looking into the girl's madness, talking with the boy about the code, and asking the father about Arthur—and hearing instead of the king at the great castle, who had been known as Poll, or Poel. The legends of his companions, the civilization itself, as the man talked of them fitted well, but the name was different. The enigma of this disturbed me not much. It was no longer Arthur I would be seeking.

To these people I couldn't make any payment, except in teaching the boy, which I was glad to do, and in telling my story. The code came dryly to my lips, there within a mile of the burnt-out castle. The boy himself had seen the knights, and took my theory into an experience more actual than my own; but he listened straightforwardly, and with respect. He was small for fourteen, but stocky, wire-haired, tough: he would be active.

In the first few days I did offer them my horse to sell, and they seemed to accept the offer, putting me at ease. But when I was fit enough to ride, they produced him again, and insisted that I keep him. Perhaps I didn't put them to great expense—five bowls of soup rather than four, another loaf every three or four days; inactive for the first time in my life, I seemed to need little to eat. Still, their charity troubled me. It was part of my thinking in those weeks, part of my dryer view, to come to see that the heroic quester, whatever self-sacrifice he shows, must depend for his career on the unobtrusive sacrifices and

support of many unheroic labouring people. I
had spent nearly two years being fed by others.

When I left, early in Lent, they were as confident of my new direction as I; and the expecta-
tion was that I would reach the fisher-lord on
Good Friday, the day of blood and all compas-
sion. The people in the settlements along the first
day of the journey knew of it, too, and turned out
with pieces of honeycomb, nuts, and the cider-
dipper. They were more elated than I; but I too
was more content than at any time in the winter.
I had my assignment, a magic and holy one. I
was thinking, too, of the summer, after the
assignment was completed; when I had freed by
some means the lord Henged from his pain, and
found my way back to my lady.

I spent that Good Friday in a snowstorm,
trapped temporarily in a steep valley whose
scarps, hidden in the driving cloud, I couldn't
hope to climb through. Even then I believed
myself to be within a few miles of the fisher-
lord's house, and persuaded myself that I
should arrive on Easter Day: that this perhaps
was God's intention—the restoration on the day
of resurrection rather than the day of agony.
But when the skies cleared I didn't know the
landscape.

Since that Easter I have had to accept that my
success may not be imminent. There was a
morning recently when it occurred to me that
this search may take years, and the best years of
my life. I was in fen country, plashing quietly

through morning fog, silent and unstirred air. Faintly, far above, was the hint of sunlight; but the marshes were grey and chestnut-brown, and featureless. With movement and action, nothing seemed to change. One almost ceased to think of progress. What I felt wasn't hopelessness, but a gentler counterpart: disappointment, and acquiescence. I was calm, and felt God not so far away: the mist was not absolute.

In God, time is not very important. When I was a boy my breath itself had the urgency of the heroic career. I saw myself enlisting with Arthur, a specific and single king, and amassing a quantity of glories. The number seemed vital: I wanted to score them up. Even now, when I think of that face in its ceremony of suffering, shrivelling and collapsing with pain, witnessed by the helpless company, I think of reducing the time he must suffer. I still feel much of the old impatience, perhaps because the sooner I can reach him the less my sense of shame, at my original failure. If I had been a wiser Percival, if I had ignored the convenient instructions to reticence, trusted the awkward impulse to pity, and asked my questions, he would not be suffering now. (But even now I do not know what questions, what form. I won't know till the time.)

Yet it is a magic situation. I'm uncertain how much Henged and his house exist in time. My spur tapped against a real enough stone; but in the confusions of the search its existence in geography begins to seem doubtful; and in all my other doubts I find myself sure that the relationship is with me only. No one can release him except me.

The stillness, in the marsh-fog, was pervasive. With a hardening of the hands and a murmur I stopped my horse, once, and listened. His reality—his snuffling breath, the bubble and suck of the gases in the marsh where he had stepped, the big rough warmth of his hide against my fingers—was vivid; the rest of the world gauze-covered, fading to grey, outlines of colourlessness. In the windless air was an assertion of futility. I listened, feeling no impulse.

I can't say certainly that things are not futile. The acquiescence had been deepening in me since the early winter, since before I reached Poel's castle; and it is still in me, and perhaps always will be. I think I do now accept that either things are truly arbitrary, an utter haphazardness of God, or their direction is likely to be too difficult for us to understand, so that they appear arbitrary though they are not so.

To some this is cynicism, and to others it is faith. Either way, we have to live with the appearance of arbitrariness. Moments of urgent purpose, fevers of vision and conviction, will come to us, more often to the lucky ones. In the possibility of meaninglessness, codes may be more important than ever: we have to interpret our days—that is how God made us, and to interpret isn't a voluntary choice—and interpreting will by definition offer meanings, or codes which assume meanings. I still hope to teach boys the code in which I was trained, as Mansel taught me.

When I try to explain this to skilled men, I'm often asked why, in a context of arbitrariness, I don't abandon the search for Henged and the Grail. Self-sacrifice, I have been told (even by devout men in monasteries)—self-sacrifice is foolish if the purpose and the reward are uncertain. Usually they are not trying to dissuade me from the search, but diagnosing in me a belief which I mistakenly think I lack. They see my life, as I did myself until Poel's castle, as the dedicated-heroic, motivated by the most intense guidance of God.

Actually, self-sacrifice is not harder but easier, when there is no certainty of meaning. In a blank windless world, without confident directions of our own, we are most free to respond to need outside ourselves. We are free to make that interpretation of our lives. Drawn by the agony of the fisher-lord, I am less my own man; and less futile.

The events of the days pass, now, like brushing low cloud beneath the higher pattern: they are what occurs between morning and evening prayer. Some days I am with people: helping with the sowing or the harvest, mending a house-wall, clearing up after floods. Once I have helped track down a thief, and managed to persuade his neighbours not to smash his knees and knuckles—instead, they flayed him till I thought he might die, and I must watch that lesser evil as if it were goodness.

The day deepens, its colours fill and brighten, when I settle to pray.

To address God is to address a remoteness. God doesn't blaze and touch me now, as in my adolescence, and possibly will never do so again.

His overseeing is from a high distance, like the shoals of higher cloud, or the sunlight sensed above the marsh-mist. The colours of life in prayer are colours of this world's people; and I pray for those with whom I've passed the day, and for myself; always I pray for my mother, for my lady, and for the soul of Mansel my tutor; last and longest I pray for him whom I know least, and with whom I am most identified.

In the sun, in the hard dry heat of late afternoon, I teach spear-throwing to the young men and the older boys. They sweat, grunt, massage their pulled shoulders, and are delighted.

By winter-fires I learn the local songs and stories. I sing them songs from my own country—beautiful and painful for me. Well, one can't hide from the regret: I build it up and offer it to them.

Sometimes the children kneel with me as I pray, or watch, big-eyed. I press a little girl's body to me, touch my wrist to her cheek, my cheek to her hot head; and pray for my lady Whiteflower. Pray that we may have children. Certainly, though, I understand that I may never see her again.

And the old often pray beside me. Why do I feel I shall never reach their age?

My mother, unlikely to see me again, I pray for your quiet death. Make a journey to the sea, one last time; stay the night with the fishing people, watch the weather roll in from the west, feel the width of the sky. Perhaps God will be more vivid to you there than I ever now find him. Then, hard-face, go home at peace, and no longer expect me.

My lady. . . . What can I pray for you? Believe that I haven't broken faith. I found God with you; believe now that I am directed by him in colder ways, to a unique need. And believe that if he lets me return, if I'm free after what I have to do, the earth will shake and the wet places flare with spray at the speed of my coming to you. That will be the greatest happiness God could grant me. I pray that your house is safe and your people loyal, and that they remember their training. I pray that you sleep alone and are praying for me. If not, with difficulty, jealous, I still pray for your happiness: that is part of my ordeal.

Mansel, I pray for your soul, confidently. As for your pupil, you can't have imagined his destiny, but you will understand it, with the understanding of heaven. I've walked through the ruin of the code, do you know that?—have knelt in the snow beside your frozen body whose heat had warmed my boyhood; have visited despair and indifference, beside the charred cross in the wreck of the Arthurian castle. It must be said, I no longer believe in Arthur, it being all I can manage to believe in God. But your blessing is with me, your education is employed: I'm on the finest quest, and success can only be mine. Pray for me and for Henged, that it may be sooner rather than later.

Fisher-lord, lord of the Grail, I pray most for you. The hall swells with shouting, still thousands of times; the hung wall of sound flaps in its own pain, and inside, inside your head it is silence, the grip of pain; the pain parts you from us, and from yourself. The hall pounds to our voice-beat; and we watch the age break into your

face, decades of suffering; our young father, ageing for us, thousands of times.

You don't count the times; and you are not, in
any important sense, within time. But my journey is within time, slow and baffled, but destined
to reach you at last; and this time I shall speak.
I was a boy before, and wrongly advised. This
time—I don't know the words or the outcome;
some tell me the suffering will end; others, that
it will become mine. But either way I have inter-
preted my life towards you. There is nothing else
for me to do; all other events are occurrences
only, between prayer and prayer, on the days of
my journey.

Remote one, stay within the reach of my mind;
and hasten my journey.

About the Author

Jim Hunter was born in England in 1939 and has lived there since, apart from one year in the U.S.A. in 1960-61. His publications include seven novels and a dozen critical and educational books. He has taught literature in a number of British schools, and in two of them was Headmaster. He now lectures for the Open University.

About the Series Editor

Born in 1941, Raymond H. Thompson lived in many different parts of the world before emigrating to Canada, where he is now professor of English at Acadia University in Wolfville, Nova Scotia. His fascination with Arthurian legend dates from student days. He has written *The Return from Avalon: A Study of the Arthurian Legend in Modern Fiction*, and he is an associate editor of *The Arthurian Encyclopedia*.

Pendragon™ Fiction

The Arthurian Companion
by Phyllis Ann Karr

Written in a warm and entertaining style, *The Arthurian Companion* contains over one thousand entries, cross-referenced and annotated. It is an alphabetical guide to the "who's who" of Arthurian legend, a "what's what" of famous Arthurian weapons and artifacts, and a "where's where" of geographical locations appearing in Arthurian literature. An extensive chronology of Arthur's reign is included.

5 3/8" x 8 3/8", 576 pages. Stock #6200, ISBN 1-56882-096-8; available from bookstores and game stores, or by mail from Chaosium, Inc., 950 56th Street, Oakland, CA 94608-3136.

The Bear of Britain
by Edward Frankland

A daring and brilliant effort to recreate the historical Arthur, set amid the savage confusion of the Dark Ages. Frankland's portrait of Arthur bears the stamp of truth. Not the Arthur of Geoffrey, of Malory, or of Tennyson, Frankland's Arthur is a tough Celtic warrior, the last native emperor of the British peoples as they struggle against the Saxon invaders.

5 3/8" x 8 3/8", approx. 256 pages. Stock #6202, ISBN 1-56882-102-6; available November 1997 from bookstores and game stores, or by mail from Chaosium, Inc., 950 56th Street, Oakland, CA 94608-3136.

To the Chapel Perilous
by Naomi Mitchison

This novel relates a new version of the story of King Arthur, the Knights of the Round Table, and the quest for the Holy Grail, as seen through the wide and wondering eyes of a pair of reporters working for the *Camelot Chronicle* and the *Northern Pict*. More than just a lively story, it concerns the twisting of historical truth in the interests of various powerful groups.

5 3/8" x 8 3/8", approx. 320 pages. Stock #6203, ISBN 1-56882-120-4; available 1998 from bookstores and game stores, or by mail from Chaosium, Inc., 950 56th Street, Oakland, CA 94608-3136.